NEW DIRECTIONS FOR TEACHING AND LEARNING

Robert J. Menges, *Northwestern University*
EDITOR-IN-CHIEF

Marilla D. Svinicki, *University of Texas, Austin*
ASSOCIATE EDITOR

Writing to Learn: Strategies for Assigning and Responding to Writing Across the Disciplines

Mary Deane Sorcinelli
University of Massuchusetts, Amherst

Peter Elbow
University of Massachusetts, Amherst

EDITORS

Number 69, Spring 1997

JOSSEY-BASS PUBLISHERS
San Francisco

WRITING TO LEARN: STRATEGIES FOR ASSIGNING AND RESPONDING TO
WRITING ACROSS THE DISCIPLINES
Mary Deane Sorcinelli, Peter Elbow (eds.)
New Directions for Teaching and Learning, no. 69
Robert J. Menges, Editor-in-Chief
Marilla D. Svinicki, Associate Editor

Microfilm copies of issues and articles are available in 16mm and 35mm,
as well as microfiche in 105mm, through University Microfilms Inc., 300
North Zeeb Road, Ann Arbor, Michigan 48106-1346.

ISSN 0271-0633   ISBN 0-7879-9859-1

NEW DIRECTIONS FOR TEACHING AND LEARNING is part of The Jossey-Bass
Higher and Adult Education Series and is published quarterly by Jossey-
Bass Inc., Publishers, 350 Sansome Street, San Francisco, California
94104-1342. Periodicals postage paid at San Francisco, California, and at
additional mailing offices. POSTMASTER: Send address changes to New
Directions for Teaching and Learning, Jossey-Bass Inc., Publishers, 350
Sansome Street, San Francisco, California 94104-1342.

SUBSCRIPTIONS cost $52.00 for individuals and $79.00 for institutions,
agencies, and libraries. Prices subject to change.

EDITORIAL CORRESPONDENCE should be sent to the editor-in-chief, Robert J.
Menges, Northwestern University, Center for the Teaching Professions,
2115 North Campus Drive, Evanston, Illinois 60208-2610.

Cover photograph by Richard Blair/Color & Light © 1990.

Jossey-Bass Web address: http://www.josseybass.com

Manufactured in the United States of America on Lyons Falls
Pathfinder Tradebook. This paper is acid-free and 100 percent
totally chlorine-free.

CONTENTS

FROM THE SERIES EDITORS

About This Publication. Since 1980, *New Directions for Teaching and Learning (NDTL)* has brought a unique blend of theory, research, and practice to leaders in postsecondary education. *NDTL* sourcebooks strive not only for solid substance but also for timeliness, compactness, and accessibility.

The series has four goals: to inform readers about current and future directions in teaching and learning in postsecondary education, to illuminate the context that shapes these new directions, to illustrate these new directions through examples from real settings, and to propose ways in which these new directions can be incorporated into still other settings.

This publication reflects our view that teaching deserves respect as a high form of scholarship. We believe that significant scholarship is conducted not only by researchers who report results of empirical investigations but also by practitioners who share disciplined reflections about teaching. Contributors to *NDTL* approach questions of teaching and learning as seriously as they approach substantive questions in their own disciplines, and they deal not only with pedagogical issues but also with the intellectual and social context in which these issues arise. Authors deal on the one hand with theory and research and on the other with practice, and they translate from research and theory to practice and back again.

About This Volume. This volume provides instructors who teach writing with an array of strategies and philosophies about the way writing is learned, both in the context of a discipline and as an independent skill. Focusing primarily on the best ways to give feedback about written work, the authors describe a host of alternatives that have a solid foundation in research.

Robert J. Menges, *Editor-in-Chief*
Marilla D. Svinicki, *Associate Editor*

EDITORS' NOTES

Knowledge about writing and its teaching used to be restricted to faculty in English departments. Beginning in the early 1980s, however, the writing-across-the-curriculum movement spread writing theory and practice to faculty members in all disciplines at all types of universities and colleges. Writing-across-the-curriculum was developed around a view of writing as disciplinary enculturation—helping students to learn the thinking processes of a discipline and to write like practitioners of a discipline—like physicists, sociologists, philosophers, or lawyers.

This volume's authors present a different but complementary view of writing as a mode of learning. The critical move for us, and for the writing-across-the-curriculum movement, has been from a focus on disciplinary writing to a focus on students' learning. In these chapters, both teachers of writing and teachers of other disciplines explore the use of different types of writing tasks—often called *high stakes* assignments and *low stakes* or *writing to learn* assignments. They see writing not only as improving students' communicative abilities in their disciplines but also as helping students to learn. And once faculty begin to think about students as learners, the road to good teaching is discernible. Writing not only makes *learning* more visible, it makes *teaching* more visible and brings teachers' existing practices into the foreground. The result often is a movement toward more reflective, active, and collaborative teaching as well as learning.

The chapters assembled for this volume illuminate this shift in the writing-across-the-curriculum movement from *writing in academic disciplines* to *writing to learn*. Some of the chapters emphasize research, others emphasize practice, and still others bridge the gap between the two. They offer faculty members practical advice on designing and integrating low stakes and high stakes writing assignments in disciplinary courses and suggest effective ways to respond to student writing. They also inform faculty developers and administrators as they seek to develop new programs and initiatives in writing across the disciplines.

In the first chapter, Peter Elbow provides an overview of the distinction between high stakes and low stakes assignments and between high stakes and low stakes ways of responding to student writing. He argues that high stakes assignments and responses make the most work for us and often cause the most difficulty in teaching and learning; we can use fewer high stakes assignments if we have plenty of low stakes assignments; and we can do less high stakes responding if we use plenty of low stakes ways of responding.

The notion of using low stakes writing assignments to better help students learn and teachers teach is further explored in the next three chapters. In

Chapter Two, Toby Fulwiler shows how writing weekly letters back and forth between instructor and students encourages student motivation, inquiry, and exploration. Writing class letters also allows an instructor to recalibrate course goals and assignments, increase dialogue with students, and shape a classroom community. Chapter Three, by Art Young, provides several concrete examples of ungraded writing assignments that can be used by teachers in a wide variety of disciplines. He argues that such writing helps students learn the content of the course and helps to create a classroom environment that encourages active learning and interactive teaching. Using writing assignments to help students learn material better in both large lecture and small seminar courses is the subject of Chapter Four, by M. Elizabeth Sargent. She suggests ways that peer response groups can model for students the ongoing conversation of a discipline and draw them into it, especially when assigned readings are difficult.

The two subsequent chapters shift the emphasis from low stakes assignments to the use of higher stakes assignments. In his chapter on using student writing in philosophy, Steven Fishman focuses on five types of writing assignments that attempt to balance personal/informal writing and academic/formal writing. Fishman argues that the interplay of personal and academic writing heightens student thinking and involvement and allows an instructor to write and learn alongside of students. In Chapter Six, Anne Herrington presents advice on how to develop inquiry-based high-stakes writing projects, to offer guidance to students throughout their work on a project, and to respond in ways that are regardful and informative.

The next two chapters report on research findings that suggest how best to respond to student writing. In Chapter Seven, Elizabeth Hodges describes her analysis of teachers' written responses to student essays and students' impressions of their teachers' written thoughts. She suggests practical ways teachers can respond to what they observe in their students' writing so that students can understand and learn from their teachers' written comments. In Chapter Eight, Ronald Lunsford reviews his study of teacher responses to college student writing in the disciplines and, based on that work, presents guidelines for responding to student writing. His key point is that teachers' comments should reflect their learning goals for individual students and that fewer, and more focused, comments are likely to be more effective than a large number of unfocused teacher responses.

In responding to both high and low stakes assignments, the introduction of instructional media and computer technology by the instructor offers a whole new territory to explore. In Chapter Nine, Chris Anson demonstrates how tape-recorded commentary can help teachers to play a more supportive role in the development of students' writing in different disciplines. He presents strategies for using the method along with some excerpts from students' writing and teachers' taped commentary. In Chapter Ten, Gail Hawisher and Charles Moran offer a framework for thinking about the differences between responding to students' writing on-line and off. They demonstrate that the newness of the on-line environment changes not only patterns of student learning but also teaching practices.

The final two chapters of the volume show what happens in terms of student assessment and teaching development when faculty members use high and low stakes writing across the disciplines. In Chapter Eleven, Peter Elbow suggests two ways to make the grading of writing assignments work better for teachers and students: the use of minimal grades or fewer levels of quality—not only for low stakes writing but also for high stakes writing—and the use of focused criteria for each writing assignment. Elizabeth Caldwell and I conclude the volume by suggesting ways in which faculty development programs can help to improve student learning and to foster more effective teaching through writing-to-learn programs and activities.

A closing word is necessary on the collaborative process of creating this volume. Those of us represented here circulated early drafts among ourselves. Some of us also shared drafts with our own writing groups. In addition, Charles Moran carried our chapters to a writing workshop for twenty-one teachers from the Springfield, Massachusetts, Public Schools. These teachers helped edit the final manuscript. The end result is a sourcebook that presents our collective as well as individual knowledge of and experience in assigning and responding to student writing. A sincere thanks to all.

Mary Deane Sorcinelli
Peter Elbow
Editors

MARY DEANE SORCINELLI is associate provost for faculty development and director of the Center For Teaching at the University of Massachusetts, Amherst.

PETER ELBOW is professor of English and director of the writing program at the University of Massachusetts, Amherst.

*This essay argues that we will have an easier and more productive
time with student writing if we make a distinction between high stakes
and low stakes assignments and also between high stakes and low
stakes ways of responding to student writing.*

High Stakes and Low Stakes in Assigning and Responding to Writing

Peter Elbow

As I try to understand my own experience of writing and the experience of my
students and as I try to plan my teaching, nothing has been more useful to me
than the simple and crude distinction between high and low stakes writing—
the question of how much a piece of writing *matters* or *counts*.

Assigning Writing

The goal of low stakes assignments is not so much to produce excellent pieces
of writing as to get students to think, learn, and understand more of the course
material. Low stakes writing is often informal and tends to be graded informally. In a sense, we get to throw away the low stakes writing itself but keep
the neural changes it produced in students' heads. High stakes assignments
also produce learning, but they are more loaded because we judge the writing
carefully for soundness of content and clarity of presentation.

It's obvious why we need high stakes assignments in our courses. We
can't give trustworthy final grades that reflect whether students actually
understand what we want them to understand unless we get them to articulate in writing what they have learned. If students take only short-answer tests
or machine-graded exams, they will often *appear* to have learned what we are
teaching when in fact they have not.

Am I saying that if students can't explain something in writing, they don't
know it? Not quite. That is, I acknowledge that some students can understand
something well and yet be hindered from explaining it in writing because
of their fear of writing or lack of skill. In fact, it sometimes happens that
we understand something well that we can't even explain in speech—much

less in writing. Nonverbal knowing is most obvious in realms like music, art, and dance (mathematics?), but it can occur in any realm. That is, we can know something at a felt, nonverbal level before we find words for what we know.

But even though students *can* sometimes know things they can't explain in writing, I still argue for high stakes writing. I think good college grades should reflect more than nonverbal and nonwritten understanding. They should also reflect the ability to *convey* that understanding in writing. (Conceivably we should relax this demand in music, art, and dance classes.) I hasten to add that my tough position rests on two gentler premises. We should *honor* nonverbal knowing, inviting students to use low stakes writing to fumble and fish for words for what they sense and intuit but cannot yet clearly say. And if we assign lots of low stakes writing, students are much less liable to be held back by fear or inability to put what they know on paper when they come to high stakes writing.

Students may complain, "But how can you grade on the basis of writing when this isn't a writing course?" We mustn't forget here a basic pedagogical principle: we are not obliged to teach everything we require. We don't teach typing, yet we often require it. Must we stop requiring skilled reading unless we explicitly teach it? Besides, if we require students to explain their learning on paper, we will be doing a big favor to our campus writing program and writing teachers. Writing courses only work well if students *need* writing to prosper in their other courses. (For more about assigning high stakes writing, see, in particular, Chapters Five and Six.)

Importance of Low Stakes Assignments

Writing *feels* like an inherently high stakes activity—especially because most people learn and use writing primarily in school, where it is virtually always evaluated, usually with a grade. Writing tends to be used for more serious occasions than speaking. ("Are you prepared to put that in writing?") Speech feels more like a low stakes activity because we learn it in the home and on the playground and use it casually everywhere. We don't usually think of our speech as being graded.

But speech *can* be used in formal and evaluative settings—as when we are interviewed for a job or give a talk. In fact, if we pause and reflect for a moment, we will realize that our speech is almost *always* evaluated, even if not formally graded. How we talk and what we say are probably the main basis on which people we meet look down on us or are impressed with us.

And writing *can* be used informally, even casually, and in a nonevaluative setting. In truth, if we are looking for the best possible low stakes arena for language—for using language to learn, explore, take risks, or commune with ourselves and not have our language be evaluated—writing is much *better* than speaking. Writing permits us to keep our words private or to revise them before showing them to anyone else. Speech is riskier because it is almost always heard by someone in its first bloom; it can never be taken back.

In this volume, Toby Fulwiler, Art Young, and M. Elizabeth Sargent in particular (Chapters Two, Three, and Four, respectively) describe low stakes writing assignments: frequent, informal assignments that make students spend time regularly reflecting in written language on what they are learning from discussions, readings, lectures, and their own thinking. These informal pieces of writing are sometimes done in class and sometimes for homework. These pieces are low stakes because individually they don't have much effect on the final grade. Teachers tend to distinguish these assignments by calling them not essays but *quickwrites, letters, freewrites, thinkpieces,* or *inkshedding.* (When we require students to turn in a draft of a high stakes essay a week or more before the final version is due, the draft tends to function as a low stakes piece.) Stephen Fishman and Anne Herrington (Chapters Five and Six) describe a mixture of high and low stakes writing assignments.

Because it is so ingrained to treat writing as a high stakes activity, especially in schools and colleges, I want to summarize here some of the special benefits of low stakes writing.

• Low stakes writing helps students involve themselves more in the ideas or subject matter of a course. It helps them find their own language for the issues of the course; they stumble into their own analogies and metaphors for academic concepts. Theorists are fond of saying that learning a discipline means learning its discourse, but learning a discipline also means learning *not* to use that discourse. That is, students don't know a field until they can write and talk about what is in the textbook and the lectures in their *own* lingo, in their informal *home* or *personal* language—language that, as Vygotsky famously observed, is saturated with sense or experience.

• When students do high stakes writing they often struggle in nonproductive ways and produce terrible and tangled prose. When they do low stakes writing, their prose is usually livelier, clearer, and more natural—often more interesting—in spite of any carelessness and mistakes. They don't tie their syntax in so many knots or defensively restrict themselves to simple "Dick and Jane" sentences, because they aren't worrying so much about the grade or whether they are writing exactly what the teacher was looking for. I've almost never seen a piece of low stakes writing I couldn't easily understand. But I've seen *lots* of high stakes writing that students worked very hard on that was impenetrable.

• Low stakes writing improves the quality of students' high stakes writing. By assigning frequent low stakes pieces, we ensure that students have *already* done lots of writing before we have to grade a high stakes piece—so that they are already warmed up and more fluent. Their high stakes pieces are more likely to have a clear, alive voice. And it's no small help to their high stakes writing that *we* have seen a number of their low stakes pieces. For then, when they turn in a high stakes essay that is awkwardly tangled or even impenetrable, we don't have to panic or despair; we can just say, "Come on. You can say all this in the clear, lively voice I've already seen you using."

• Low stakes writing gives us a better view of how students are understanding the course material and reacting to our teaching. We get a better sense of how their minds work. We can see better the interactions between their thinking about course material and their thinking about other realms of their life, between their thinking and their feeling. We get better glimpses of them as people.

• Probably the main practical benefit of frequent low stakes assignments is to force students to keep up with the assigned reading every week. When students put off the reading till an exam or major paper is due, they learn much less from discussions and lectures. And when only the teacher and a few diligent students have done the reading, the whole course tends to lose steam.

Responding to Writing

When we assign writing, we can trust that we are helping students learn more and probably even write better. But when we respond or comment, we can't be so confident. The news from researchers is not encouraging. They have discovered how often teacher's comments are not clear, how often comments are misunderstood by students even when they are clear, and how often comments cannot be trusted (for example, the teacher writes, "You should omit this section," or, "You need a comma here," or, "This hypothesis has been discredited," when in fact many or even most authorities would disagree). Researchers have trouble finding good evidence that our comments on student writing actually help students learn more or write better. (Elizabeth Hodges is one of these researchers, and in Chapter Seven, she gives us interesting and practical glimpses into the essential sequence of events: the teacher's reactions to a student paper, that teacher's actual comment on the paper, and the student's reading and understanding of that comment.)

These sobering results are not really so surprising once we stop and reflect on the conditions in which we write our comments and the conditions in which students read them. After all, we write comments in great quantity— working slowly down through thick stacks of papers on our desk. It is often late at night and we are usually in a hurry. And truth be told, we are often writing in a discouraged or downright grumpy mood. Writing comments on papers and exams is a *major* portion of the "academic writing" of most academics, yet it's not the writing we really care about. It seldom has much effect on our careers, and we seldom do any revising of it. No wonder it is seldom our best writing. And let's face it: it's not feasible to write our comments really slowly and to revise them carefully. We are surely going to continue to write comments fast, late at night, and not always in the best mood. Still, we can learn to do it better—thus the efforts in this book.[1]

Even when we write clear, accurate, valid, and helpful comments, our students often read them through a distorting lens of resistance or discouragement—or downright denial. (Don't we sometimes read responses to our own articles by professional reviewers through similar lenses?) When students read what we write, they are usually reacting at the same time to all the past teacher comments they have received on their writing. The most obvious example of this is that students tend to take almost *anything* we write as criticism—even if we are just asking them a question or making an observation, or even making a low-key statement of mild praise. ("I'm curious how you managed to be so dispassionate on such a controversial issue," or, "I was interested that you were able to quote from a book that I didn't assign." "Uh oh, I'll never do those things again.") And when we include a grade with our comment, we increase the likelihood of a distorted reading—sometimes no reading at all!

What discouraging news. But I think we need to hear it. It helps us ask some very practical questions as we respond to student writing: "Am I wasting my time with this comment? What are the chances that it will be understood as I intend it? That it will help?" Perhaps we could adopt the principle of our better-paid fellow professionals: "At least do no harm." When we *assign* writing, at least we do no harm.

Continuum Between High and Low Stakes Responding

In the face of this bleak situation, I call again on the distinction between high and low stakes. But here I am emphasizing a continuum with many intermediate points. Just as important, it is also a continuum from the least responding to the most responding.

Zero response (lowest stakes). When I am clear and honest with students about the fact that I need to require more writing from them than I can comment on, I help them fairly quickly get over any feelings of deprivation or resentment. Most students come to appreciate the chance to write with the knowledge that they will be *heard* but will not have to deal with my response. In fact, many teachers require *some* low stakes writing that they don't even read. Students can appreciate and benefit from the freedom of this private writing. (See Sargent and Elbow, Chapters Four and Eleven, respectively, on ways to deal with private writing.)

Minimal, nonverbal, noncritical response. We can note effective or strong or correct passages by simply putting a straight line underneath particular words or phrases or alongside longer sections. (Teachers often use check marks in the margin for this purpose, but I find straight lines are more specific markers.) I can respond in this way virtually as quickly as I can read. Almost every student needs some encouragement, and some students on some occasions need lots. Even in very poor pieces of writing, certain parts are always better than others; students benefit from having them pointed out. To find strong points, even in weak writing, is a skill that will help us improve student learning and writing.

Supportive response—no criticism. There are usually things that students do well that are hard to point to with simple straight lines (for example, "You chose a good approach to your topic," or, "You write with a clear and lively voice.") Whether we call it praise or positive reinforcement, the fact remains that this kind of response does the most good with the least effort. That is, we are most likely to cause learning and least likely to do harm if the message of our response is, in effect, "Please do more of this thing you are already doing here." We are *least* likely to cause learning and most likely to do harm if we give the message that is all too often implied in critical feedback: "Start doing something you've never done before."

Descriptive or observational response. An example of this response: "You begin with an anecdote from your own experience; then show us how it throws light on your academic topic. Then you make your case—which really rests on a process of definition—showing what fits and what is excluded." One of the hardest things for student writers is simply to *see* their own text, to understand the logical and rhetorical strategies they have used. Neutral and noncritical observations can be very effective because students don't need to resist them.

Minimal, nonverbal critical response. Just as quickly as we can read and put in straight lines, we can also put wavy or wiggly lines underneath words or alongside passages that are unclear or problematic or wrong. It's remarkable what a strong sense of our readerly presence and response we can give to students when we note five or six phrases or passages per page with straight and wiggly lines: they get a felt sense of what is working and not working for us.

Critical response, diagnosis, advice (highest stakes). This is our meat and potatoes—what we tend to assume is our main job. Obviously, we often need to give critical response to help with learning and to explain the basis of poor grades. But my premise here is that the higher we go on the continuum, the more we need to ask the crucial pragmatic questions: Is this comment worth it? How much response do I need? How much criticism will be useful? What is the likelihood of my effort doing good or harm?

I don't mean to suggest that we can just mechanically match low stakes responses with low stakes assignments and high with high. Obviously, we will often *mix* levels of response—in particular, mixing praise and criticism. Even the *highest* stakes assignment merits some praise.

Nevertheless, it pays to notice the natural links between levels of assignment and response. That is, the lowest stakes response (zero response) goes most naturally with low stakes assignments: when the writing doesn't much matter to the final grade, we can afford to withhold our response or criticism. Similarly the highest stakes response (critical response) goes most naturally with high stakes assignments: if our judgment of a student essay will have any significant impact on the final grade, we are obliged to explain any criticism we have. This critical response carries the highest stakes for many reasons: with critical response, we have to worry more about whether we are wrong or unsound; critical response is more likely to misfire or do harm because of how it is received—even if it is sound; and critical response is likely to cost us more work and more uncertainty. In contrast, low stakes minimal responding requires the least time and effort from us, requires the least expertise from us, takes the least time away from our teaching of the subject matter, and is least likely to turn teachers and students into adversaries.

I am not trying to stamp out critical response; I'm just arguing that we should use less of it—and use more minimal and low stakes response instead. Note, for example (and this is another case of mixing), that we can use plenty of low stakes praise without giving up criticism—without pretending that a piece of writing is better than it is. For example, we can write something like this: "Your paper doesn't work very well and the worst problem is confusing sentences. I often couldn't understand you. Nevertheless you do have plenty of clear sentences and I've marked particularly strong ones with a straight line. To work on your serious problem, try to figure out what you were doing when you wrote those strong sentences—and do more of that." It might seem hard to find examples of good organization in a disorganized paper, but not if we set our mind to it. For example, we can write: "I got lost a lot as I read your paper. It has big problems with organization. But I've put straight lines along several paragraphs that hang together just fine, and also lines *between* several paragraphs where they follow well and your transition works fine. Give us more of that! You've shown you can do it."

It is important for us to realize that we don't need to feel *guilty* if we use lots of low stakes and minimal response—especially if we are not teaching a writing course. Assigning more writing, using less response, and using more praise doesn't mean leaving out all criticism or lowering standards. Students need the experience of writing a great deal and getting minimal and low stakes response because they tend to associate writing with criticism and high stakes. If we are not so much teaching writing as *using* writing to teach something else, it makes particularly good sense to use lots of minimal and low stakes response. When we assign a piece of writing and don't comment on it, we are *not not-teaching*: we are actively setting up powerful conditions for learning by getting students to do something they wouldn't do without the force of our teaching.

Conclusion: Concrete Suggestions

• For high stakes assignments, it can be very helpful to require a draft a week or more before the final version. Teachers handle drafts in a wide variety of ways depending on their circumstances and styles. At the very least, we can just collect drafts and not comment—simply checking that they are done— thus forcing students to carry their thinking through two steps. Of course, if our circumstances make it feasible, it is good to give comments on a draft. When we comment on a draft, our response becomes almost automatically low stakes, even if critical: we can write suggestions for revising rather than just an autopsy. (Notice in Chapter Six how Herrington describes the production of an essay that has very high stakes but one that students work up to along a path of lower stakes drafts and comments on those drafts.) It is probably worth cutting back on the amount of responding on *some* assignments for the sake of giving students at least one experience of feedback on a draft aimed at a revision. If we can only do this once, it's better to do it in the first half of the semester—with the goal that students can internalize some of our responses when they work on later high stakes assignments. But commenting on drafts may be more feasible than some teachers think: if we give good responses on a draft, we can make do with just a quick verdict on the revision (perhaps using the kind of grid that I suggest in Chapter Eleven).

• Even when we are commenting on a final version, we can frame our comments in a forward looking way: instead of saying, "Here's what didn't work," we can say, "Here's what to work on in future papers."

• I find it easier to comment on important assignments if I get students to turn in a short reflective *cover letter* or piece of *process writing* with the assignment itself. I invite something informal, even handwritten. I ask them to tell me what they see as their main points, how they went about writing and what happened, which parts they are most and least satisfied with, and what questions they have for me as a reader. Reading the cover letter usually helps me decide what to say in my comment. Often I can agree with much of what the student has said, and sometimes I can be more positive about the essay than the student was. Students may have difficulty at first with this self-reflective writing, but it promotes a skill worth working on. It gives them practice in trying to see their own thinking more clearly. (Herrington gives good examples in Chapter Six of cover letters for a mid-process draft and a final draft.)

• I find commenting much easier if I read the whole piece before making any comments except for straight and wiggly lines. I save lots of time by reminding myself that students can seldom benefit from criticism of more than two or three problems. Therefore, the most crucial decision in commenting is *which* problems to focus on, and I can't make that decision till I read the whole paper through. Most of my bad commenting comes from jumping in with marginal comments as I am reading: I am more likely to waste my time on something that turns out to be a minor issue, or make some passing remark that the student misunderstands, or say something that's actually wrong ("You obviously don't understand x," when later on it's clear that she does understand x), or get caught up in a little spasm of unhelpful irritation. If I settle for just making straight and wiggly lines, these serve me as a map when I glance back over the paper after I have read the whole thing and I am trying to decide what are the few main things I need to say. (In Chapter Nine, Chris Anson points out an exception: when we put our comments on a tape cassette, we may want to tell the story of our reactions *as* we are actually in the process of reading. Yet Anson also points out that even for this kind of responding he sometimes does better by waiting till he has read the whole piece.)

• As Hodges points out in Chapter Seven, when we return papers to students with our comments attached, it's a great help sometimes to ask students to take five minutes right then and write us a short note telling what they heard us saying and how they are reacting to it. This helps us learn when we are unclear or when students misinterpret our words or react in ways we don't expect.

• If we are writing comments where the stakes aren't too high, we can save time by waiting till we have two pieces in hand, read them together, and write only one comment on both. The comparison is often pedagogically useful. ("Notice how much clearer your point was on this paper compared to that one [or how much more carefully you argued]. What helped you?")

• Though it sometimes costs me a few more words, I try to avoid an impersonal "God/truth voice" in my comments. Almost anything that we might say in response to a piece of writing is going to be affected by our own point of view. Even the main ideas in our discipline are arguable. If we are willing to say, "Unconvincing for me," instead of "Unconvincing," students are more likely to pause, listen, and think—instead of just resisting, or else unthinkingly giving in to authority. Besides, magisterial shorthand words like "Awk" are often extremely unclear. I have been trying to learn to write more accurate translations like, "I stumbled here," or, "I'm lost," or, "Wording feels unprofessional," or, "Too slangy for my ear," or, "Can you be less roundabout?"

I sum up this chapter with that useful dictum "At least do no harm." Think how much good we do in assigning lots of writing, especially lots of low stakes writing. But this approach is only feasible when we realize that we can get by with far less response and criticism than we usually assume.

Note

1. It interests me as a writing teacher to note that though our commenting on student papers is undeniably "academic" and indeed "professional" writing, it is often very casual: we often write in incomplete sentences and use lots of "I" and "you." I'm not saying that these features make our writing bad or unprofessional or unacademic. I'm just pointing out that many academics unthinkingly *assume* that casual informal writing is not academic and should not be used by students.

PETER ELBOW is professor of English and director of the writing program at the University of Massachusetts, Amherst.

Writing weekly letters back and forth between instructor and students harnesses the energy of a familiar form and friendly voice in the service of classroom community. No other writing assignment the author has ever devised has the motivating power of these letters.

Writing Back and Forth: Class Letters

Toby Fulwiler

When people write about anything, they learn more about it. Often, they learn more than they intend—about what they know, what they don't, and where they need to go next. Often, the same draft that answers some questions poses others. Serious writing, in other words, is a dynamic, unpredictable thinking process, seldom a straight line, seldom complete in one draft or sitting. School assignments, however, often cut this complicated process short, asking that one draft or sitting to answer old questions, but not raise new ones. Too often in school writing, stakes are high, the pressure on, the deadline close, but opportunities for dialogue and revision few and far away.

> *Dear Classmates,*
>
> *Welcome to "Studies in Composition and Rhetoric." During the semester we'll explore the historical development and current state of teaching writing within the field of English studies. We'll look at selected contemporary issues, including cultural literacy, action research, and writing across the curriculum. Finally, all of us will examine process of our own composing—how we learned it, how we do it, how we change it.*

Writing letters back and forth with your students increases dialogue, suggests rethinking, and encourages rewriting, yet the stakes remain low. Weekly letters promote the give and take of learning rather than the finality of testing and measuring.

All letters in this chapter, both mine and the students, are authentic and reproduced with permission; some have been edited for clarity, brevity, or anonymity. My thanks to the students in my graduate seminars from 1993 to 1995 for permission to use their letters in this chapter.

Each week I invite you to write a letter to me about ideas related to our readings, writings, and class discussions. Make your letter honest, lively, and personal, while still addressing matters of intellectual and emotional concern about writing and teaching writing. At least once, include your classmates as your audience, making copies for all to read and respond to.

Each term, I write weekly letters with one of my classes, composing my syllabus as a letter, requesting letters back. I would write letters with all my classes if I had time and energy, but I don't. I ask other classes to keep journals and share selected entries with me to which I informally respond.

I will write a letter back to all of you (the whole class) each week, mailing it on Monday so that you will have read it by Thursday. In this letter I will address some, but not all of the concerns you raise collectively in your letters to me. (In fact, I have written this syllabus as a letter to suggest a possible model for length, style, and form.)

I happen to teach English and so use letters in both my undergraduate and graduate writing courses. But were I a teacher of history, nursing, or natural resources, I would also use letters (as does my chemistry colleague, Michael Strauss, who assigns them in organic chemistry). Letters work in all subjects where instructors and students care about each other's thoughts, see curriculum as exploration, and are willing, at times, to negotiate who is the learner, who is the teacher.

Thanks for writing back to me in our first class. Ten of you report feeling pretty good—if somewhat confused—four are anxious, one ready to drop. (Hmmm.) Let me share back some of your first impressions of the letter assignment:

Steve—I'm not comfortable with a "letter" being indicative of my writing on a scholastic level.

Mary—I like to write letters, and am a little concerned about turning a private pleasure into a public product.

Sue—I like how the letter format makes your syllabus seem like part of a conversation and our writing back, part of the conversation.

Gustav—I think I'm a little in the dark about your intentions here.

In my letters back, I share fellow students' concerns by quoting students selectively, not worrying about citing each student in every letter, trusting time to even things out. When reading a set of student letters, I look for themes, highlight common questions, and try to quote people fairly, not out of context. After a few weeks of finding *their* ideas featured in *my* letters, nearly all the students enjoy the larger intellectual community that shared ideas create—and they like, especially, the notion that their weekly questions and concerns become part of the course agenda.

Liza—I want to learn more about portfolio assessment and how to incorporate it into a classroom.

Pike—My main interest is seeing how writing can be applied in real world situations.

Larissa—Though I've taken several writing courses, I really don't know how one teaches—let alone learns—to write well.

Everyone knows how to write letters. Graduate students, undergrads, and instructors have written, received, and read letters of one sort or another all their lives. In the public schools, students saturate their classrooms with unassigned letters—called notes—with or without teacher approval. Letter writing is as natural and easy as writing ever gets.

Todd—Previously, writing two pages for a class would have been as bad as pulling teeth, yet here I just rattled it off painlessly.

Michelle—If I were to teach a high school literature or writing class, I would have the students . . . write a brief letter explaining their lives, interests, dislikes, lifestyles, language styles, course expectations.

Early on, I ask the students for blanket permission to quote from their letters by name, suggesting they mark overly private passages "don't publish," but trust that otherwise I will cite them fairly. Their trust is usually warranted, though occasionally I have made mistakes:

My apologies to the several of you I quoted out of context last class; I meant to survey the wide range of class reactions to Britton and Berthoff; I did not intend for this sampling to substitute for a full scale debate of the readings.

Letters imply equality, more or less. Writer and reader make a tacit pact to converse and explore in conversation, each with a turn to say, a turn to respond: the response is part of the assignment, the assignment part of the response. Being equal increases the chance of being honest.

I'm sorry we ran out of time at the end of last class—I didn't allow enough time for reading to each other or for articulating your revision plans. I really want you to tell me (by writing a note on the back of your draft) where you plan to go next on your paper—I always read this before formulating my own comments, trusting you know better than I what to do next. We'll do better next time.

Letters are invitations to share, explore, query, and continue talking. Letters are good places to try out ideas, see how they are received, listen to reactions. If an idea is questioned, reformulate it, expand it, or bag it. (Hey, it was just an idea.)

Sue—Am I a writer? Perhaps this class will answer that question.

Stephanie—I'm hoping this course will unlock some kind of secret door and I will begin to write for myself and then enjoy showing my writing to others—which so far in my graduate career has not been the case.

Kathy—I've never felt like a "writer," would never call myself a writer, and am sometimes shocked to see my own words in print.

Letters don't have thesis statements. Or if they do, it may be an accident. Nor do they need to assert claims or arguments or hypotheses or propositions that then need to be supported, proven, or documented in MLA, APA, or CBE style. In fact, a letter that is all thesis and support puts a damper on exploration and dialogue. Of course, a letter will sometimes lead to a thesis, and that's okay, too.

Todd asks, "Do you always teach writing the same way?" Well, I'm really not sure. My only honest answer is yes and no. In all writing classes I aim at the same things—to improve writers' knowledge, strategies, and confidence levels. The difference between first-year and advanced students is where to start, what to expect, how far to go. So, essentially, my objectives with your class remain the same—to help you write better and feel better about yourselves as writers.

In exams, term papers, and lab reports, when you admit you are confused or don't know something, you leave yourself vulnerable to criticism, ridicule, and low grades. In letters, you admit, share, explore, and debate your uncertainty.

Jaime—If teachers teach the same course the same way won't it get awfully boring?
Joanne—I think teachers always teach the same course, but same, by the way, doesn't necessarily mean boring.
Trish—Yes, I think we all do teach the same way . . . the same pulls, the same urges, the same drives . . . your quest is always the same: to get the student to a place they were not before.
Gustav—I can't really shed any light on this subject.

Letters let you have it both ways. (What do I mean by that?) Letters encourage doubt and uncertainty as well as candor (of course, other forms allow for these things, too—personal essays, for instance—but letters actually promote them). You can *assert* in one voice then *question* your assertion in another and not be penalized for your confusion. Too often in thesis-driven writing, you are expected to have it only one way (or to pretend to have it only one way), to have one thesis to prove or support—especially if you are a student writing a paper. But letters invite the back and forthness of the doubtful mind, accepting the paradoxical and contradictory way the world seems to work.

(Well, Todd, my answer to you makes me wonder if my objectives are always the same in teaching literature courses—to improve readers' knowledge, strategies, confidence levels. But I do have different agendas in introductory survey courses than in narrowly focused classes for majors, don't I?)

Most people write letters in their natural writing voices: first-person pronouns, contradictions, personal asides, digressions, humor, slang, expletives. . . . I prefer dashes to semicolons, ellipses to transitions, sometimes sentence fragments, other times endless sentences.

> *Kathy—I've finally realized that my letter to you is teaching me something—the letter is really more for me than you, isn't it—or am I wrong? (How could I be wrong!)*
>
> *Toby—Ask yourself if you learn best from listening to yourself or listening to others? Reading other's writing or writing yourself? If you're anything like me, you'll answer, "Well, it sorta depends."*

The letters let me restate class objectives in a way that often needs doing some weeks into the term. In fact, letters allow me to refocus and redirect the course of the class throughout the course of the class.

> *Whether you plan to teach or not, in this class, your writing is part of course content—an object of study: how I assign it; how you approach it; how I respond to it; how, where, when you compose it; how we negotiate it; how we share, assess, and learn from it.*

Peter Elbow (1981) talks about "good-enough writing"—writing that conveys information in a sufficiently clear, but not elegant manner, that accomplishes approximately what both writer and reader need for the moment. Letters can be like that, too—one-draft good-enough writing that makes a good enough case and doesn't need to be revised, edited, and worried to death—but here, too, there are exceptions.

> *Mary—Is it necessary or advisable to revise these letters to you?*
>
> *Toby—No, not unless you care to. However, I'll admit that I revise my weekly letters to you because addressing fifteen specific people at once gets pretty complicated. . . . So I revise to be clearer, more clever, more honest, more comfortable—I care very much about how my writing represents me and my ideas (& I'm also aware of how closely you examine my words for clues to my values, beliefs, biases—hey, I'm the guy who grades you—I don't blame you).*

When people write letters to people they trust, they worry less about conventional correctness and more about the matters on their minds. Letter writers don't try to make mistakes (at least I don't), but when they do it's no big deal. But letter writers do try to avoid misunderstandings (at least I do).

> *So, Mary, my institutional authority (!) makes me as careful in my way as you are cautious in yours. But ultimately, I revise more to be honest and clear than safe: I love language, form, genre, style, image, rhythm, wordplay, voices, and so I end up revising and editing every expression intended for public consumption, even memos, e-mails, and class letters such as this.*

Peter Elbow (1981) also talks about "no-big-deal writing"—writing that's accepted as exploratory and tentative and doesn't commit the writer to a whole lot, that's not contractual nor set in cement or stone. No-big-deal writing: try it out, try again, again. Letters can be that part of a conversation where you say, "Maybe," or, "No, that's not what I meant at all," or, "Hmmm." What Peter now calls "low stakes writing."

> Laurie—*I write, I am. Yet, writing is pain . . . an ordeal.*
> Trish—*I am beginning to realize my writing might be better if I began creating a paper trail.*
> Sam—*I am confused. And you know what? I am finally realizing that confusion and learning are integral to each other.*
> Edis—*It is impossible to remove ourselves from our writing. But it is possible to hide our thoughts, to hide ourselves behind a rhetorical screen.*

Letters are short on organization and development. Not necessarily, of course, but because they are often one-draft productions, their organizational patterns are most often associational rather than logical or chronological. And they are long on readability and candor. Not necessarily, of course, but because they are often written to a real person rather than for a grade, there's little point in pretension, deception, or bluff. They are informal papers with a real audience.

> Carol—*At the end of class you said that we should not be "critics" of reading that we have not fully read or understood. I disagree. I think we should be critics of everything we read, or do, or say to a certain degree.*
> Gustav—*I am still roaming in darkness—is there any source of light?*

Letters substitute well for quizzes because they include reactions to and explorations of weekly reading assignments—but without a sense of judgment. (You can't write much about what you haven't read—after a while it begins to show.) Letters have the advantage in allowing writers to respond to readings on their own terms and in causing less anxiety. In classes where I use letters, well-prepared students become the rule rather than the exception (there are always exceptions). In addition to asking for general responses, I sometimes ask for letters that address particular issues.

> *As you finish Jim Berlin's chapter on the current status of composition studies, examine our seminar syllabus, readings, classroom practices, and writing assignments; explain why Berlin would classify our class as expressive, cognitive, or social epistemic.*

Letters expand the possibilities of journals. *They are journals with an audience*—informal, searching, tentative, honest, sometimes emotional. Authentic journals are for the writer's self, not the teacher reading over her shoulder, so honest journal writers are always in a bind when instructors collect their journals. Note that letter writers try harder than journal writers to make thought communicable: writing "Dear Toby" makes all the difference, because they know I don't know what they know. And it makes a difference for the letter writer, too, as such forced shaped thought often leads to interesting places.

> *Edis [a teaching assistant]—Most of my English 1 students don't like journals: Some will [ask] for more in-class directed journal writes (just tell me what you want), while others will tell me they cannot write under the pressures of time and class environment (it's not natural).*

Letters promote classroom community. Not necessarily but usually, as everyone enjoys the freedom to explore anything about the course he or she wants to. When students and instructors write to each other, they hear each other better.

> *Jennifer—Upon reading the other students' comments I felt myself a part of a "community of thinkers." . . . I was actually surprised that so many of us do not view ourselves as writers.*

Letters encourage playing with conventions, with language, with my reader (who I'm trusting will accept my play and, in turn, play back with me). I write in various forms and voices to suggest that in letter writing there really ain't no rules.

> *Gustav—In Switzerland our undergraduate classes were more formal—not at all like this. It has been hard getting used to. Writing was expected to be formal too, and to be finished and carefully documented when you handed it in. There was no changing it or revising—and no playing with your voice. I'm starting to like the play.*

Letters are alternate modes of assessing learning. More to the point, they allow you to witness (and assess if you wish) the process of learning, as do journals and classroom conversations.

> *Meanwhile, some are worried about what counts in here: The letters count—I expect fifteen by week fifteen; but it's the doing of them that counts, not their conventions, content, form, or style. In the same way, your journal doesn't count—at least not for me—as I don't intend to read or measure it. But keeping one will provide material from which to write letters, find ideas for papers and research projects, and help your mental health to boot. (No promises, but that's what mine does for me.)*

Letters invite letters back. When you write letters, you expect a reply—not a grade, but an honest-to-goodness reply. You start a dialogue with no necessary right answer, conclusion, or end in sight. Your letter invites mutual exploring, questioning and answering, possibly a meeting of two minds—collaborative learning.

Look, you either write the letters or you don't. If you miss one or two, no big deal. If you miss more, what's the problem? Exactly what and how you write are your business, that you write is mine. But, believe me, your reactions to the readings, class discussion, research projects, as well as anything else related to the course helps me teach better.

Letters lower your expectations. (It's just a letter.) A letter is a sample of what's on a writer's mind at the moment of writing, not of his or her comprehension or literacy or worth. There can always be another letter—better, more thoughtful, more complete, literate, clever, or profound. Letters leave doors open. The only fair assessment of this particular assignment is quantitative.

Laurie—I was relieved to read in your letter that it was the doing of the letter that counted, not the content, style, etc., though admittedly, I have a very hard time believing that.

Each week, it takes me about two hours to read student letters and write mine back—longer for the set of thirty-two, the largest class in which I have assigned letters. They work especially well with once-a-week graduate seminars, where they seem to add an extra class meeting by promoting out-of-class dialogue. (And they work especially well to relax graduate students who become especially anxious about their developing professional voices and selves.)

This time I had the urge to respond to nearly every one of you individually—but, as usual, I just didn't have the time. I can tell that, now, in your fifth letter to me, most of you are accepting—even liking—the letters back and forth as another way to advance our seminar (frankly, I'd have been surprised if this hadn't happened, human beings talking to each other in writing).

E-mail letters, in which i don't capitalize, are something else again—very useful and a little different from these weekly paper letters. E-mail letters seem to evolve naturally, now, in all courses where I share my e-mail address. I encourage students to open e-mail accounts in order to correspond privately with me as well as more easily with each other. In addition, if students want more responses from everybody, I invite them to subscribe to the class listserv, which allows them write to me and their classmates simultaneously. When students send me an e-mail letter, I do write back individually—briefly but personally.

From: toby fulwiler <tfulwile@moose.uvm.edu>
To: kristina m. <kristina@moose.uvm.edu>
Subject: new paper
On Mon, 6 Nov, kristina wrote:
   Hi! E-mail is fun and saves me printing ribbon! I can't wait to get my paper back from you tomorrow. I really enjoyed writing the one on my language autobiography.

It's rough because I have a lot more to include, but this is the first time I've worked with prose snapshots. It's amazing how they speed up the writing process, since there's no need for lengthy transitions. It almost feels as if I'm cheating or taking the easy way out, but it isn't as easy as it looks.

yes, i know, and i love the cheating, cutting to the chase that the snapshots allow. but as you probably already know, they only work when you craft them as you do conventional paragraph writing. right now, i'm writing a chapter on "letters" all in snapshots for a book about writing assignments. wish me luck, too.

From the first letter on, my students and I add P.S.'s to our letters. We do this in order to share information that has absolutely nothing to do with the class itself—though it has a great deal to do with getting to know each other as real people who have lives beyond the classroom. In a seminar in which people must trust each other enough to read and respond helpfully to each other's writing, I want us to know each other.

P.S. The hardest thing about February, for me, is the distance remaining until motorcycle season—at least another month, more likely two. It's not the cold that stops me (my motorcycle has a windshield, heated handgrips, electric vest—this is, after all, Vermont); what stops me is the ice—ice gotta be gone from the roads for two wheels to stay up—just in case you wondered.

At term's end, I move the letters from an informal to a formal assignment—or, as Peter Elbow would say, from low to high stakes—and expect now to see more focused, deliberate, and crafted writing examining themes, patterns, and concerns of a term's worth of correspondence. I request "an Edited Edition of your collected letters with an introduction to provide context and excerpts to explain their meaning or value."

Stephanie—What emerges from these letters, as I re-read them, is a sense of my world as one big hologram. Everything is connected in some way. If you break a hologram into pieces, any one piece will reflect the same pattern as the whole together: this is how I compose my life on these pages. What I always thought was a hindrance to my learning—my personal and emotional sensitivity—is really the core of my learning.

The edited edition of the letters is a real term paper of sorts, providing an evolutionary overview of each writer's semester journey—the results of which often amuse, enlighten, and surprise writers who by term's end have forgotten what they wrote two months ago (so, there really is a pattern to my thinking after all!).

Stephanie [a teacher intern]—A good example of [my emotional sensitivity] is found in the letter of February 18:

This week I am starting to decompose, to fall apart again, to dissect myself.
Are my expectations too high, or am I really just a poor student and a poor
teacher? Sometimes I feel things more strongly than I think them.

Yet, ironically, in writing about these emotions, I not only share and validate them, but actually start to recompose myself. This same letter ends:

Being a teacher doesn't mean you feel secure all the time. . . . You shouldn't
feel as if you've failed just because you haven't performed well on a par-
ticular day—besides, those are the days I usually learn the most.

In a course with regular informal writing and with multiple drafts of formal writing, a writing portfolio is the most reasonable mode of assessment. Each portfolio contains all the accumulated work of the semester, including responses from me and classmates, to which is attached a self-assessment letter. To communicate this term's end assignment briefly and clearly, I move to a memo.

To: Classmates
From: Toby
Re: Portfolio assessment
    Your final portfolio should include the following assignments:
—drafts 1 & 2 of the collaborative research reports
—drafts 1 (objective), 2 (subjective), & 3 (mixed) of your classmate profile
—drafts 1 & 2 of your collected letters
—selected journal entries (optional)
—a cover letter explaining how you would like me to read your portfolio & what it
reveals about your writing and learning.

Of all my writing assignments, weekly letters receive the highest marks from students for their combination of personal, social, and academic worth. After the first few weeks, in which students test the form to see how I respond, what I expect, how they work, their acceptance of the letters as a meaningful assignment is near unanimous (nothing about teaching is really unanimous).

Stephanie—These letters are a great way to organize our reactions to the read-
ings & class, a good way to pose questions, express anxieties, inform each other about
our individual struggles, and reflect as a community on common problems and ideas.
    Sue—After reading all 14 of my letters, I can see how much I learned about
myself, my writing, our class.
    Mary—Overall, these letters served as a journal for me. They allowed me to open
up and reflect on my academic experience as well as my personal life. I'll miss not doing
them.
    Dan—To write the letters, I had no choice but to think about my own writing—
I had never actually sat down and thought of myself as a writer before. I can identify
points in those "forced" letters where I see myself maturing as a writer.

Gustav—This class—these letters—helped me find pleasure in expressing myself in wild ways, playing with my voice, laughing with it, crying with it!

The disadvantages of letter writing? Each week, your students need to write, and some won't like that. Each week, you need to read what they write. Each week, you need to write back. Each week, you will hear student concerns that make you uncomfortable or may cause your course to change. And if you are anything like me, you will miss not assigning letters in your other classes.

Reference

Elbow, P. *Writing with Power*. New York: Oxford University Press, 1981.

TOBY FULWILER, professor of English at the University of Vermont, directs the writing program, teaches introductory and advanced writing classes, and conducts writing workshops for college instructors across the disciplines.

The purpose of assigning writing that will not be formally graded is to assist students in learning subject matter and to create a classroom context that encourages active learning and interactive teaching. This chapter gives three examples of writing-to-learn assignments and suggests ways teachers can respond to such writing.

Mentoring, Modeling, Monitoring, Motivating: Response to Students' Ungraded Writing as Academic Conversation

Art Young

One of the most important uses for writing in educational settings is as a tool for learning and for classroom conversation. When writing is used in this way, the emphasis is not on the communication of knowledge already learned, nor on writing as an instrument for testing, nor on the effective expression and formal presentation of ideas. Rather, the emphasis is on writing as conversation, speculation, and problem solving. Writing used in this way enables the primary purpose of the classroom, whether the learning of physics or the learning of history, to proceed in a way that actively engages all the participants in the development of knowledge. There are a variety of ways to respond to such writing, but the purpose of response should be to encourage further thinking and further conversation among participants in the classroom conversation, not to correct errors and provide commentary and grades on the quality of the writing.

In what follows, I provide three examples of ungraded writing assignments that are used successfully by teachers in various disciplines and at a

I wish to thank the student writers and their teachers for granting me permission to quote from their writing. I have changed their names to protect their identity. And a special thanks to the students in my writing groups at Clemson University and Michigan Technological University who provided me with feedback on early drafts of this essay: Reid Austin, Sean Clancy, Tony Dendy, Dickie Selfe, Laura Stanton, and Zhigang Wang.

wide variety of institutions. These examples are illustrative not exhaustive, and they suggest strategies in a progressive order: from those ungraded writing assignments that require little classroom instructional time or out-of-class time from students and teachers to those that are more fully integrated into course goals and thus require a more extended time commitment from students and teachers.

Five-Minute Essays

One example of a writing-to-learn assignment is the *five-minute essay* (or *freewrite,* or journal entry). At the end of a class period, whether it be a lecture, lab, or discussion, the teacher asks students to write for five minutes about two things: (1) what they have learned in class that day and (2) what questions and concerns they still have. A mechanical engineering professor at Clemson University uses this technique in his sophomore-level statics course. The professor collects the responses, reads them quickly before the next period, and responds individually to students. Here is the five-minute essay of one student, let's call him Michael, with the teacher's response (in bold italics):

1. *The method of joints is a way of analyzing structures (trusses) by observing the forces at each joint in the structure. For every structure a system of equations can be developed to solve for the forces at these joints. If the structure is partially constrained, the structure has more equations than unknowns and will collapse under force. A statically indeterminate structure is likely to be rigid but the forces of the joints cannot be found because there are more unknowns than equations. Only a statically determinate structure will be rigid and have the minimum # of elements, thus producing the same # of equations as unknowns.*

joints where forces are calculated

2. *Is a statically indeterminate structure always rigid?*

If it is internally indeterminate, yes. If it is due to excessive external constraint, such as

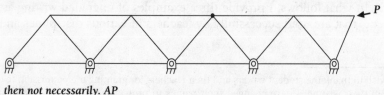

then not necessarily. AP

Although we might not understand the technical language, we can see the process at work here. Michael puts the main points of this day's lecture in his own words. In the act of reviewing his notes, Michael realizes he doesn't understand something and asks a question. The teacher ("AP") then responds specifically to Michael's question. Michael is reviewing what he does know and what he doesn't know and then appeals to the mentoring teacher for help.

Indeed, most of Michael's summary may still be in the teacher's words, and in the act of transposing these ideas, in class, under time pressure, and with the teacher as audience (and therefore a different activity than simply recopying notes to study for a test), students begin to make this unfamiliar language ("indeterminate," "statically determinate") and way of problem solving their own. Some teachers, under time pressures themselves, will frequently skip the first part of the assignment ("summarize in your own words") and simply ask students to write out questions for further discussion. Although this technique is undoubtedly better than not asking for questions and concerns, my experience leads me to believe that it does not generate as many purposeful questions. In the example quoted above, Michael writes, "A statically indeterminate structure *is likely to be rigid* but the forces of the joints cannot be found because . . ." (emphasis added). As Michael recalled the main points of the day's lecture, his attention was drawn to the word "likely." What does this word mean in this context? Does it mean that there may be cases when a statically indeterminate structure may not be rigid? Thus the visible synthesizing (that is, the writing out) of the material under study has led Michael to ask an informed and important question. When teachers notice students asking good questions, they are monitoring whether course material is being understood. You have to be informed to ask informed questions.

Teachers like this technique for a variety of reasons: it puts them in frequent contact with students—what students are learning and what they are having difficulty with; it encourages questions that might not be voiced in front of the entire class; it promotes good listening skills because students know they will have to synthesize what they hear in their own words; it provides opportunities for students to become confident with using technical vocabulary and with putting new concepts in their own words; it promotes good student-teacher communication. Indeed, in this one example, all of the language arts are used to learn and think about mechanical engineering: listening: both students and teacher hear one another and respond; writing: students and teachers write to each other informally but purposefully; reading: students and teacher read each other's writing; speaking: teachers and students converse with one another on paper, but often with increasing frequency, orally, both in and out of class; and visual communication: teachers and students use a variety of graphic forms—drawings, graphs, formulas—as needed to facilitate their conversation.

Teachers have experimented with variations on this assignment to meet their own needs. In large classes, for example, these writings are collected, but because of time limitations, the teacher does not respond to each individually but rather gives an oral collective response at the beginning of the next class—"Here is what *I* learned from reading your five-minute essays"—and goes on to discuss issues and questions that emerged frequently or that are particularly provocative. Other teachers do not collect the writings, at least not daily, but ask one or two students to read theirs at the beginning of the next class period—as a way of summarizing the previous lecture and seeing what questions still exist. Teachers occasionally ask students in groups of four or five to read each other's writings and then select one question to bring before the entire class. In this way, students hear what three or four other students think was most important about the previous lecture and hear what kinds of questions are being asked, and the teacher ensures that good questions that are of interest to several students get taken up by the whole class. One teacher gives closed-book and closed-notes tests but allows students to use their collection of five-minute essays during tests. Students are thus motivated to be more attentive listeners and note takers and then to write really useful five-minute essays. The more accurate the lecture summaries and the more perceptive the questions (including teacher response, if any), the more valuable they will be to the student at test time.

The most important thing to remember when using such writing assignments is that their purpose is to create a classroom environment that supports active learning and interactive teaching. Thus teachers should be flexible when using such writings and not see them as an end in themselves. Such writings, as already suggested, can be used at the end of a class period, but they also can be useful at the beginning and middle of classes or even done outside of class. And teachers can respond to the student writings in different ways at different times: individual written response, collective oral response, students' responses to each other in pairs or groups, and so forth.

This model of response generates a feedback loop (teachers respond to students, students respond to teacher and to each other) that encourages mentoring, modeling, monitoring, and motivating. Students who ask real questions and get individual responses appreciate the mentoring involved in such a process; students who see their teacher change a lecture ("After reading your five-minute essays, I realize we need to spend some more class time on statically indeterminate structures") see the effects of honest communication on the teacher's monitoring of student learning; and students who get useful answers to questions, who feel free to ask questions when they are confused, and who are rewarded for asking such questions (by something as simple as class recognition—"Michael asked a good question in his five-minute essay last time, and I want to spend some time talking about it") become more motivated to learn by participating in a dialogue about statics and by making a contribution to the professional conversation about mechanical engineering. Although they are novices, they have entered the conversation under the tutelage of more experienced members of the profession—their teachers.

There are three other general principles that teachers should use in implementing such writing-to-learn assignments.

• First, the writing should be integrated into the daily life of the class—to assist in creating the interactive environment. Such writing will not work for most students and teachers if it is assigned, written, and then not discussed in class, not used to further class goals. Such writing must have social purposes within the classroom—to create a community of scholars learning about the subject being studied. If the writing is not central to the ongoing work of the class, if it is perceived by students or teacher as an add-on to the important work of the class, then it will receive the peripheral attention it deserves.

• Second, students should be told why they are being asked to do such writing. Students sometimes see all writing as busy work, as just another mark to go into the grade book, so the reasons for asking them to do such writing should be explained as clearly and as frequently as appropriate. And then students should be involved in further shaping the assignments: Are the assignments fulfilling their purpose? How might they be made more useful and effective?

• Third, teachers should assign such writing only if they are eager to read it—only if they are eager to enter such an interactive mentoring relationship with the students. To assign such writing and then to see reading it and responding to it as necessary drudgery will work against the goal of creating an effective classroom environment.

Such writing and reading must not become busy work for either students or teachers. If it does, it is time to restructure the class and its assignments.

Poems

Another example of a writing-to-learn assignment is a poem. Yes, a poem. Teachers have been experimenting with ungraded poems in such courses as accounting, biology, entomology, mathematics, and women's studies. Such assignments suggest that students can benefit from writing creatively in any course because such writing can generate new and fresh perspectives on the subject under study, encourage students to play with language and ideas, and increase the quality and quantity of student-teacher interaction. The purpose of such assignments is not to make the student writers accomplished poets but to provide imaginative and playful connections to learning opportunities.

When asked to write a brief poem (less than a page) on earthquakes in a geology class or on schizophrenia in a psychology class, students will, of course, write a range of poetry—some serious, some humorous, some rhymed, some unrhymed. Let me give you a particularly playful example from an "Introduction to Entomology" class at Clemson. The teacher had spent considerable time in this large lecture class attempting to persuade students about the value of insects to the ecological well-being of the planet and to human life. About half-way through the term, she asked students to write a poem for homework on some aspect of insects. Here, in part, is what one student wrote:

BUGS, BUGS, BUGS!!!!
creepy, crawly, greasy, grimy,
nasty, smelly, gooey, slimy
big bugs, small bugs,

black bugs, red bugs,
bugs that can jump or walk,
bugs that can swim or talk—"bug talk"
I see bugs on the wall
I see bugs at the mall
. . . .
bugs in my rug, bugs in my bed
bugs that I like best are bugs that are DEAD!

On first reading, this student, obviously, was having none of the teacher's interpretation of insects as valuable, fascinating, essential. But as the teacher read further, she picked up the good-natured theme of many students ribbing the teacher. In another poem, she read:

To some these loathsome creatures
May solve great mysteries
But I would be much happier
If we could wipe them from history.

And in another:

Such a pity was the death of Big Bubba [the ant]
He left behind millions of kids and a mate
But that's the price he had to pay
For walking under my size eight.

Because there is no way to grade these poems, at least in the traditional sense, many of these students took risks that the freedom from grades afforded them. There are no right or wrong poems. Scientific writing (about entomology, for example) strives to be nonfiction, based on fact, believable. Poetry writing strives to be fiction, a product of the imagination, an exploration of what should be. So rather than concentrating on how to respond to these student poems, this teacher concentrated on understanding their value in shaping her classroom environment. To her, they said that most of students employed humor, irony, and language play; and they used metaphor and analogy for expression and thought. They exercised their imaginations; they reached out to readers—their teacher and each other—and they expressed concerns and opinions that related course materials to their lives.

Without any prompting from the teacher, students shared their poems with each other, passing poems from one class member to another before class began. By their giggles and exclamations and nods of appreciation, they were responding to each other. The teacher asked that some be read aloud to the entire class, and all that were read received encouraging and good-natured feedback. In addition, the students requested that all of their poems be collected and desktop published in booklet form and distributed to the whole class, and with the help of the students themselves, this was done.

In this case, the teacher collected and read the poems, but there was no need for her to respond to each one individually. In not knowing how to respond to them in any traditionally critical sense, she found a way to give the most meaningful of responses. By her actions, by what she said, by her body language, she was telling the students how much she enjoyed reading their writing. By allowing class time for the poems to be read, she placed significant value on them as learning and communication tools. By desktop publishing the collection and posting a copy on the tackboard outside her office, by giving copies to other teachers who requested them, she was responding to these writers. As a scientist, she modeled the imaginative daring and playfulness that is a component of science. As a science teacher, she realized that this poetry writing experience and the enthusiastic response it generated in entomology had increased the motivation of the students to contribute to the course, especially when, a little later in the term, they asked again to write poems on another subject having to do with entomology. And she accomplished these things without any written response to these student writings.

Letters

Another teaching strategy that encourages active learning and conversational give-and-take is the letter assignment. In this assignment, students exchange letters in pairs and respond to each other. The teacher may join in this assignment and be a letter partner as well, especially if there are an odd number of students enrolled in the class. The purposes of this assignment are similar to the five-minute essay, but additionally, it promotes cooperative learning among class participants and a more sustained inquiry into important issues generated by the students themselves. Like the five-minute essay, the letter format encourages the use of the personal voice and informal language in support of higher-order critical thinking skills and the development of more formal language skills and a scholarly habit of mind. One strength of this assignment is that it asks students both to generate the issues to be discussed and to respond to each other's assertions and questions (rather than the teacher generating the questions and doing most of the responding) and thus to create and model the academic conversation that generates knowledge in most all areas of study.

Here is the context for the letter exchange in my most recent Victorian literature class, a class that enrolls primarily junior and senior English majors and minors. Toward the end of the semester, students had one week to read the novel *Heart of Darkness* by Joseph Conrad and to read the critical introduction to this particular edition by Cedric Watts. Part 1 of this assignment, the first letter, was written to a partner about the problems encountered in interpreting the novel, and it was written before the novel was discussed in class. It could be handwritten and was to be about 200 words long. Part 2, the response letter, in which students suggested possible answers and perhaps raised other issues to be discussed, was written following a week's class discussion and needed to be typed and be about 500 words long. Each letter was to be submitted in two copies, one for the letter partner and one for me, the teacher. Students knew as well that there would be a final exam question on *Heart of Darkness*.

Here are excerpts from the exchange between the students Cookie and Kelly:

> Dear Kelly,
>
>   My first question comes from the end of the story where Conrad writes that the Thames "seemed to lead into the heart of an immense darkness." What do you think he's talking about exactly? "Heart of Darkness" usually refers to Africa, I know, the Dark Continent as well as the dark forces dormant in men's souls. To me, the story seems to be about discovering those forces as we are taken out of civilization, so isn't it ironic that he uses this reference now when the story is back in civilization? I ask this because at the beginning of the story he uses as much dark imagery describing London as he does for Africa. It doesn't seem to be that they are leaving the lighted safe city for the dark jungle so much as they are going from a place where "darkness" is underneath to where it comes to the surface.
>
>   This brings me to my second question—do you think they go to Africa and learn to be corrupt or that they are corrupt and use Africa as the excuse? . . . Is the darkness there out of civilization, or do they bring it with them?
>
> > Cookie

Cookie's letter to Kelly refers to specific passages in the novel, attempts to synthesize these issues around the central metaphor of the novel—the "heart of darkness"—and then asks specific questions related to the apparent contrasts between England and Africa and between civilized and primitive societies. Cookie is suspicious that all is not as it appears on the surface of things during her first reading, so she contextualizes her questions in terms of her own experience with the novel. She describes for Kelly what she understands as well as where she has questions. Cookie has given Kelly a lot to think about. A week later, Kelly responds, after having read a prompt from me that said in part: "Take the letter a classmate has given you and consider it carefully, review *Heart of Darkness* and our class discussions about it, and then respond to your classmate with a thoughtful note of explanation and exploration. Explain where you can, and where you are not sure of particular aspects yourself, explore reasonable possibilities."

> Dear Cookie:
>
>   In his introduction to *Heart of Darkness and Other Tales*, Cedric Watts writes "the darkness of the book's title refers to many kinds of darkness: moral corruption, primitive savagery, night, death\ignorance, and that encompassing obscurity of the pre-rational which words seek to colonize and illuminate" (xvii). The last line of *Heart of Darkness*, "seemed to lead into the heart of an immense darkness," corresponds to Marlow's comments only a few pages into the novel when he says of England—"and this

also has been one of the darkest places of the earth." Here Marlow seems to use dark imagery to describe land in its primitive state, as it is used to describe the Belgium Congo. Yet I believe that the more important implication of the imagery of darkness is the corruption and evil in every man. This evil is found in all men, but lies dormant, controlled by civilization. That Marlow begins by saying that England was once dark and concludes by saying that it is still dark reveals that he believes that it is not simply the land which is dark, or that civilization ends darkness, but that the darkness remains a part of each man on every continent. Marlow describes "the wilderness that stirs in the forest, in the jungles, in the hearts of wild men" as if the wilderness is removed by civilization (140). But the actions of the English men belie his belief that efficiency has saved them and removed the darkness. Efficiency, Marlow's word to describe the importance of civilization, merely hides the darkness. The moral corruption that seems to exist in Africa also exists in England; it is merely kept underground, only whispered about.

Several examples of corruption in England are present in the novel. It is in England that the Ivory Company makes its plans to send Englishmen into the Congo to take ivory. It is in England where Marlow, who believes lying to be abominable, is forced to lie to the Intended. He rips the words "Exterminate all the brutes!" from Kurtz's report thus aiding continuation of sending Englishmen to Africa to "enlighten" the Africans with Christianity. . . .

In Africa, the English men are not more corrupt than they were in England. . . . The men are internally corrupt and being in Africa simply allows their corruptness to manifest itself externally as well. The men no longer have to whisper. Because they are more powerful than the Africans, due to weapons and explosives, they are able to prey on them without fear of reprisal.

Your friend, Kelly

Kelly's thoughtful response speaks directly to the issues raised by Cookie, and she provides several informed observations about the nature of the darkness that she reads about in the novel. Although she writes a personal letter to Cookie and addresses Cookie's very specific concerns about the novel, Kelly's language and critique are thoughtfully academic. Let me share with you my interpretation of just the first paragraph of Kelly's letter, that is, the kind of intellectual work I see going on in her writing.

Kelly begins her letter by integrating a relevant secondary source, Cedric Watts, into the discussion, but she soon will use this quotation in support of her own purposes. She then focuses on the exact quotation about the Thames that Cookie used—"the heart of an immense darkness"—and shows that this statement by Marlow at the end of the novel is consistent with his statement at the beginning of the novel, that England "has been one of the darkest places on the earth." And then she does an insightful reversal, the central meaning of the heart of darkness metaphor and therefore the book is not Watts's prerational, primitive savagery or even Marlow's own troubling attempts to locate evil in a geographic place. Kelly writes: "Yet I believe that the more important implication of the imagery of darkness is the corruption and evil in every man." She goes on, using specific references to the text, to answer Cookie's questions by doubting the reliability of Marlow's narration. Marlow may see the darkness "in the hearts of wild men," but his own story seems to show that it is equally in the hearts of civilized men. But in civilization, the darkness ("moral corruption") is "only whispered about." Kelly returns to this wonderful metaphor in the final two sentences of her letter: Europeans "no longer have to whisper" in Africa, where they dominate the people brazenly and loudly with "explosives."

Kelly has collaborated with Cookie in generating knowledge about the novel; she has given Cookie significant ideas to think further about; and she has helped her teacher gain a better understanding. And when she and Cookie are asked to read their letters aloud to the entire class (which some students will do), her insights, derived from her ability to read difficult texts and to write about them, can be useful to many others. Kelly and her classmates are joining the conversation of literary scholars about this classic but controversial novel. And they are doing it in a way that respects the scholarly tradition—the conversation that goes on in the classroom and outside of it in many nations and times—but does not simply parrot the traditional interpretations of published scholars. Indeed, as you might suspect, in most cases, the experience of writing these letters is most valuable for the writer herself or himself. In our busy lives and under normal circumstances, Cookie and I may have spent ten or fifteen minutes reading and considering Kelly's letter and then been appreciative for the insight it afforded us. But Kelly has written her way into an experience with *Heart of Darkness* that is likely to remain with her long after the Victorian literature class has ended.

As we consider how best to respond to students who write such letters, this is a crucial point to remember. *The primary value of the assignment is to the writer and not to the readers; it is an opportunity for active learning and problem solving.* Thus, in responding, we do not primarily judge the writing on how well it communicates to readers (or how well it conforms to the form of the personal letter), but rather we value and affirm the writing and learning revealed in the students' writing and encourage further inquiry.

When we integrate writing into our classes as a tool for learning the subject matter being studied, in such diverse classes as statics or entomology or Victorian literature, we are changing the setting in which school-based writing occurs. In most school-based writing, we ask students to write for us in order to improve their writing or to have their knowledge of certain material assessed, and we judge that writing and make suggestions for improvement based on these goals. But writing-to-learn changes this setting by changing the purpose of the writing, the audience for it, the context in which it occurs, and the appropriate response from readers. In the letter example given here, the topic for the writing is generated collaboratively (by the teacher who assigned the novel and the fellow student who asked the questions); the class discussion is informed by questions that the students have already asked themselves and each other—and ones they will have to consider further when they sit down to write their second letters; the purpose of the writing and the class discussion is for students and teacher to work together to help themselves and each other build a better understanding of the novel and its connection to human experience; the audience for the writing is first a fellow student, second the teacher, and third the entire class. Because I assumed that with just over a week to read the novel, discuss it in class, and write about it, most people (certainly including me!) in that time frame would not write an important critical essay publishable in a scholarly journal, I chose the genre of the personal letter in which students would do this speculative writing. And in the matter of response, each writer received an almost immediate and individual response to the questions raised in her or his first letter—a response that often took another writer as much as two or three hours to compose.

Grading and Response

But how do I, the teacher, respond to ungraded writing-to-learn? If I am not going to grade it, judge it, what am I going to do with it? Well, for me, there is no one answer that covers all situations, as you might expect. My answer depends on the purpose and the context of the assignment. I do keep the admonition in this chapter title in mind as I respond: mentor, model, monitor, and motivate. Here is how I handled the student letters in my Victorian literature class (but I will do it differently next time because the context will be different—the students, their questions, their writing, the class discussion). First, I read the letters in sets of four (two letters—questions and responses—by each pair of letter partners). I put no marks on the letters themselves (there were thirty students in this class—so sixty letters to read and respond meaningfully to). I made notes about the letters on a separate sheet for my own use. After reading the letters, here are some of the ways I responded to them.

• I modeled for the students how I read their letters. Just as I interpreted Kelly's introduction for you above, I did a similar interpretation on one of their letters before the entire class. I demonstrated that their writing deserves the same close reading as other scholarly writing.

• I selected excerpts from several students' letters to be read aloud by the authors to the entire class—sometimes a couple of paragraphs, sometimes a sentence or two. I was looking to get many issues about the novel before the entire class—but in their voices. I wanted them to see that people read this novel in very different ways.

• When students exchanged the second letters, I made class time for the letter partners to read them immediately and to chat briefly about them—to express appreciation, to ask more questions, to respond orally to each other, to consider an issue they jointly would like to bring to the entire class for discussion.

• By using student writing as the focus for class discussion, I made their writing about *Heart of Darkness* central to the knowledge they and I were gaining about this literary text. The writing was not an add-on, written only for the teacher and not important enough to take up class time.

• I asked them for a brief written response on how the assignment worked for them, and then I discussed these responses with the class, telling the students that the next time I taught the course I would assign *two* sets of letters (about six weeks apart). Many students made this suggestion because they felt that only after the experience did they realize the value of it—and they believed that they would be even more motivated to engage another literary text through the letter exchange now that they had experienced the entire process.

• I asked students to include these letters in their portfolios of writing, which I collected, read, and responded to in writing at midterm and again toward the end of the term. Thus the letters were read in the context of students' other course writing: freewrites, formal critical essays, and creative exercises such as poems and parodies.

The first time I read the student letters, my concern was to read them in such a way that they enabled the ongoing academic conversation of our class in developing student knowledge and experience with Victorian literature. I read the letters in pairs, and I was looking for ways to respond to our collective experience with *Heart of Darkness*. My second reading of their letters was in the context of their individual portfolios. Thus, the first time, I read sixty letters by thirty students about one novel. The second time, I read about twenty pieces by a single student writer about numerous literary texts, representing his or her intellectual engagement, development, and contribution over the course of the term. In reading students' portfolios, I put no comments or grades on individual pieces of writing, but rather made as assessment about the quality of each person's work as viewed in total—with allowances made for the fact that some writing-to-learn activities will lead writers down blind alleys and off into areas of no immediate import—opportunities for discovery do not always lead to discovery. During the course, the only student writings I critiqued by making specific comments on the texts themselves were the rough drafts of formal essays—comments that I hoped would be useful in the revising process. Thus, although I made no attempt to judge the student letters in the traditional sense of assigning an A, C, or F, I did evaluate the letters and the rest of each student's writing in the context of their entire contribution to achieving individual and course goals.

Conclusion

I am still experimenting in using ungraded writing in classes in which I must issue a grade and in which most students expect regular graded feedback. There is a tension here that may never be satisfactorily resolved. But my experiences with teachers and students in courses across the curriculum, from accounting to zoology, and from Victorian literature to entomology, convince me that writing has an important role to play in most classrooms as a tool for learning and as a tool for generating classroom conversation about academic issues.

Art Young is Campbell Chair and professor of English and engineering at Clemson University in South Carolina and coordinates Clemson's communication-across-the-curriculum program.

*Peer response groups can help students learn material better in both
large lower-division and small upper-division courses in which difficult
readings are assigned and in which students learn to participate in a
disciplined written conversation with each other about those readings.*

Peer Response to Low Stakes Writing
in a WAC Literature Classroom

M. Elizabeth Sargent

When students regularly write about the assigned readings for a class and then
read and respond to what their classmates have written, they often can learn
the concepts and subject matter of a course better and remember it longer;
such peer response work can model for students the ongoing conversation of
the discipline and draw them into it.

Most undergraduates don't conceptualize an academic field as an ongoing conversation that members of that field gradually learn how to listen in on,
then to enter and perhaps contribute to. Students are much more likely to
think of a field as a body of information "out there" one needs to master; as
soon as you have that body of information inside your head, you become qual-
ified to give it out again as a teacher. Of course, that simple linear schema (of
knowledge being passed from one generation of scholars to the next) isn't completely inaccurate: we all know how much information or terminology or theory or experience we often need before certain conversations begin to make
sense to us. But the notion of an international network of people keeping such
conversations alive and growing and changing—as opposed to a list of fairly
stable facts or concepts or key texts—is foreign to all but the most alert and
sophisticated undergraduates.

Admittedly, undergraduates—particularly in lower-division courses—
could only enter into such conversations in rudimentary ways. But my experience with peer response groups leads me to believe that even such
rudimentary participation in the ongoing conversation of a particular discipline can help students learn the material of the course better and remember
it longer—and put what they have learned in a more useful and legitimate
context.

The peer response strategies I describe in this essay, however, were developed not because I understood all of the above but only because I was under stress. I was in my first year at Western Oregon State College with a teaching load of four courses per quarter (thus, twelve courses between September and June). Three preps per term was the norm, but four was not unusual. Each term, I had two large introductory required literature sections with an enrollment of fifty to sixty students in each; then I usually had two writing courses with an enrollment of twenty-five students in each. When I combined that teaching load with my belief in the value of writing-to-learn and my obvious inability to read all the informal writing I assigned (I required students to bring to every class fifteen minutes of writing in response to the reading for the day), the result on my part was panic and exhaustion. I was willing to admit that my students might have to do a lot more writing than I could ever read and comment on before their writing and thinking would ever improve, but still I was uneasy at the thought of having *no one* read and respond to what they had written. So I decided to have them read *each other's* writing.

Now, I'm committed to what necessity originally plummeted me into: I can't imagine teaching literature without this conversation between students—and between me and them—going on all the time. Like most such commitments, it required a leap at some point across a logical gap (I'm using Michael Polanyi's terminology [1958] here); I was afraid I would simply land myself in a ravine with broken bones, but there was something pursuing me from behind, so I jumped anyway. All that follows is the story of where I landed.

Although I use peer response groups in literature classes (both the large introductions to drama, poetry, or fiction for nonmajors and the small upper-level courses for majors), I think most of the strategies would work—with alterations and adjustments for a particular discipline—in any writing-across-the-curriculum (WAC) class that required difficult reading assignments. Peer response groups have made it possible for me (1) to assign more writing than I could do otherwise (without peer response, I could only assign this huge quantity of writing if I had most of it be private writing, in which case students might not take it as seriously, and (2) to have students spend more time inside each other's heads and thus learn more from each other about the course material than could ever happen otherwise. (There are obvious links here with recent work on collaborative learning and problem solving in the classroom; I won't focus on those links in this essay, except to mention here our growing realization of the power of student-to-student learning.)

Inkshedding Set-Up: What I Need to Do Before Putting Students into Response Groups and Expecting Them to Know What to Do

When I first tell my students that they will be reading and responding to the writing of their peers, they moan, "I can't correct someone else's writing—I haven't had my writing course yet," or, "I'm bad at writing [or grammar or spelling or whatever they mean by writing]"—or (most angrily), "You're the teacher, not me—you should correct everyone's writing."

But these complaints usually come from those who haven't been listening or who have missed the first day or so of class, for by that time most students in the class have done some inkshedding for me and have begun to experience the crucial distinction I want them to make between *correcting* and *responding*. I try to model in *my* responses to their first two pieces of writing how this conversation on paper can work and how different it looks from grading or correcting or evaluating. What it should look like, as one student put it, is "talking onto the margins of the other person's paper." The focus should be not on surface error but on content, on students helping each other become alert, sensitive, close readers of literature.

Inkshedding is a Canadian term, linked primarily with James Reither's work (see Craven, 1995, Coe, 1993, Pare, 1993, Reither and others, 1994, and Reither, 1995), and a term I'm using these days because it makes students laugh and because it's usefully unfamiliar. It doesn't carry whatever baggage the word *freewriting* seems to carry with it. (Unused to the concept of focused freewriting, students will often protest, "How can this writing be 'free' if I'm told I have to write about a specific topic, like figures of speech in an Emily Dickinson poem?") Inkshedding starts with and uses freewriting but always puts it in a communal context. Inkshedding has been connected from the start to academic tasks and the social construction of knowledge: writing responses to readings or to papers at conferences as a way of focusing one's thoughts, then sharing them with others, participating in an intellectual conversation. Because freewriting to many students means private, personal, or journal writing, they often resist using it for serious and public intellectual work. But the assumption from the start when people inkshed at a conference or in a class is that others will read it, that passages from it will be excerpted and distributed to all participating inkshedders in order to advance or feed into the discussion they're having. (The first Inkshed Conference took place at St. Thomas University in Fredericton, New Brunswick, Canada, in 1984, but I have only recently discovered how exactly inkshedding parallels what I have been trying to do in my literature classes since 1989). Inkshedding is an effective tool for allowing everyone to talk at once and for getting quieter students, the ones who rarely speak up in class discussion, to share the smart ideas and good questions they so often keep to themselves.

So, if students have shed some ink on paper for me during the first two class periods, they realize inkshedding is intense, steady nonstop exploratory writing that won't be graded or marked down for surface error; it's meant to get them thinking and to leave the track of their thoughts on paper for *others* to see and work with. They also realize that a fifteen-minute inkshedding is "required" in response to the reading for the day and that I might refuse to accept it if I'm not convinced, skimming through it, both that they have *done* the reading and that they have made a serious effort to engage with it (that is, just praising the reading or reviling it in general terms won't cut it—they need to ground their responses in the text and point to particular passages). I warn them that they usually need to do some preparatory work before they begin writing, to gather quotations to refer to or look back through the text, and that the writing itself should be strenuous—it should feel as if they're running uphill. (If they have done a lot of freewriting in high school and enjoyed it precisely because it felt easy, they may resist for several weeks the energy such exploratory writing requires.)

I often ask them to use a literary term as a way into the text, as a lens through which they can see more going on in the text. (In any field, one could ask students to use a key concept or word to organize their response to a reading assignment, thereby pushing them to try out any difficult technical vocabulary necessary to that area of study; sampling these written pieces can help an instructor discover quickly whether or not students understand the terminology they're being asked to use.) I also distribute a list of other writing-to-learn strategies and ask students to try at least ten of them (see Sargent Wallace, 1994) in order to find out which ones help them enter into, interact with, question, and remember the readings most fully.

Before asking the students to respond to each other's work, I have to figure out how to put them into groups as well as model what I'll want them to do in those groups. So I collect and respond to at least two pieces of inkshedding from each student during the first week, one written during the first class (I often ask them to tell me about one play or story or poem that has mattered to them and why) and the other written after the first reading assignment.

With fifty-plus students per section, that's a lot of reading at the beginning of term; but I discipline myself to read the first batch with only a highlighter in hand, the kind students use to mark up their textbooks and help them remember what's important. Like them, I use yellow or orange or green or blue or pink—never red, the color of error. I make sure to suggest the parallel to them: I'm highlighting the lines that jumped out at me, insights I wanted to remember or observations that helped me see something in the text I hadn't seen before. It's my way of pointing to what seems strongest or most worth keeping in that piece of writing, an idea or a phrase that they could perhaps develop further or build on. Students' fresh responses to the readings often catch details the literary scholar overlooks; however, the students usually don't realize the value of those responses or know how to sort out what's obvious or even misguided from what's original, startling, or worth exploring at greater length. The teacher's role here, in helping students recognize which passages from their inkshedding contribute to—advance—the collective conversation about a particular text, is essential.

On a few of these inksheddings, the effort to highlight at least one sentence presents a challenge; so I hunt for and highlight the least vacuous sentence. Over the years, however, my determination to continue this pointing and to model it for my students has increased because the occasional dull, lifeless first pieces usually come from the most frightened students, the ones with the worst experiences with academic failure and ridicule and with the most bottled-up intellectual energy inside. They're playing it safe. It can take more than one term for trust to develop, but once they realize they can risk exposing the thoughts and questions in their heads, such students often bust out in surprising and capable ways.

Because these first two pieces don't usually get read by other students and because I make clear to the students from the start that inkshedding is not private (we do occasionally do private writing in class for a few minutes over difficult issues—it helps discussion, but I don't collect it or ask students to share it with each other), I make a habit of sharing with the class some of the most intriguing lines, the most striking interpretations or convincing, detailed readings. Near the beginning of term, before the students know and trust each other, I generally read these out anonymously. Often I'll use a particularly negative or questioning passage as a lead-in to a lecture, never as a way of ridiculing the student's resistance, but as a way of showing how a strong negative response or difficult question can help open up our reading of a text. Once they realize that even strong negative reactions, if they are grounded in the text, are acceptable, students are usually willing to grant blanket permission for their responses to be shared or quoted from, with themselves identified as author, throughout the rest of the term. Obviously, if even once the instructor betrays the trust represented by that permission, ridiculing or condemning a response publicly, both the trust and the permission will be withdrawn. I do make negative comments when they're necessary, either privately in the margins of particularly careless or inadequate pieces or to the class as a whole if I see a recurring problem in many of the written responses—but I never single anyone out publicly.

I'm getting ahead of myself here, however. Let me go back to the two pieces I read from each student at the beginning of term. One of the two—as I said above—I usually read with highlighter in hand, writing no comments or very few. On the other, I continue to highlight, to point to, specific lines or paragraphs, but I also write comments in the margin or at the bottom, responding primarily to the content (comments like, "You may be on to something here—I've never paid attention to this particular passage before or thought of reading the story this way, but I think it works; it connects with the earlier scene on pg. 0 and also helps me account for several other puzzling details, like Y and Z, that I could never make sense of before. Thanks!"). Whether my comments agree or disagree with points the students made, I try to ground them in the text we're reading, giving page references and specific lines or scenes to support my ideas. Further, because I want students to be able to identify and feel the force of stylistic devices in the works we read, I point to such devices when they appear in student writing ("I love the parallel structure building here," I might say, or, "The alliteration works well in this line." Because students usually have no idea they have committed acts like "parallel structure" or "alliteration," they might interpret such comments at first as negative criticism—research tells us they read *most* faculty comments on their papers that way, no matter how they're worded—but I gradually get them to realize that parallel structure and alliteration, two of the concepts I hope to teach, can be good things, and why).

Obviously such comments take time, and I can't do them for all fifty students all term long. My goal on these early responses is, first, to model how students can respond to each other's readings and, second, to make sure every student receives at least one inkshed back with a written conversation starting in the margin. They certainly are not to be correcting each other's *writings*, but they can quarrel with each other's *readings* as much as they like—as long as they tie everything they say to the text, to a specific page number, line, or scene. I ask them to carry on a conversation with each other in the margins or at the bottom of the page. They are required, in both their inkshedding and in their marginalia on someone else's piece, to ground their comments in at least one passage, giving the page number so they can go back to the text and weigh their own interpretation against their colleague's in case they disagree. They are never to play teacher with each other, but to converse as equals about the assigned texts.

There are several ways to manage this kind of peer response in a non-writing class. Let me just suggest two: the first for a large class, the second for a smaller one. Obviously, the larger the class, the more tightly one has to organize and stay on top of the peer response process, until the students begin to take over and manage the routine themselves.

Peer Response in Large Introductory Classes

I use my readings of the first two pieces to assign students to groups of seven or eight each; my early judgments aren't infallible, but they give me a sense who the strongest readers and writers are. I try to make sure at least one or two more experienced readers are in each group to push the thinking of the others. I don't feel guilty about doing this: as we faculty all know, the best way to learn something is to teach it, and the students with stronger backgrounds in literature have a lot to share with their colleagues as well as a lot to learn from them.

I ask the students to establish a rotation schedule for serving as *reader* for their group, a task each student will probably need to perform three or four times during the term. That is, for each class, students bring fifteen minutes of exploratory writing in response to the reading for the day. They may be asked to use that inkshed in a variety of ways during class, but at the end of the period, they must turn it in to the assigned reader in their group. That reader will take all the inkshedding home to read and respond to, writing marginalia according to the guidelines mentioned earlier and completing a brief report for me on that batch of student pieces (see Exhibit 4.1 for the form I created to structure this process). The assigned reader for the day is especially directed to write marginalia on her *own* piece, as if she were a different person (I tell the students that they *are* different people after they have read the readings of their colleagues, and they should have a lot to say to *themselves* when they look back at what their first reading was before they were exposed to anyone else's). Generally I reproduce the report form in some bright color, like orange, and ask that all the pieces be folded inside it; these must be returned to me by the next class period. The assigned reader knows that I will be reading three things closely: her initial inkshedding, with her marginalia; her report form; and her marginalia on the readings of her group members.

I record my responses to all three with a check, check plus, or check minus; but if the third task is inadequately done, I return the entire set to the reader to be redone and resubmitted. I don't want students getting their inksheds returned to them with no or skimpy written comments. Although occasionally I will dip into pieces by other students in the group, especially if the assigned reader alerts me to problems or particularly puzzling readings, responding to seven or eight of these packets at top speed takes me a full hour, so I try to discipline myself not to read more than one additional piece in each batch. I cannot read everything, and the process has taught me that the students learn a lot by reading and commenting on each other's work, even if they don't catch everything I might have caught and responded to. I keep records only on students who are missing responses (they are allowed to miss one week's worth without penalty); that saves me from having to check off every response from every student each time.

This rotation of readers ensures that I read closely roughly the same amount of exploratory writing from each student during the term. They all know when I will be paying the closest attention to their writing, so I might expect them to goof off and write carelessly the rest of the time—but my spot-checking convinces me that this rarely happens. Perhaps they begin to enjoy the process itself, to enjoy hearing what their peers made of a difficult poem or short story, and to want direct responses to what they made of it themselves. In short, they seem to forget about me as a reader, at least most of the time. Occasionally, I come across a question like, "Do you think she ever reads these?" If I see it, I write "Yes!" in the margin. But on the whole, the students begin to police themselves and to give a hard time to group members who aren't contributing or pulling their own weight. Further, they're more honest with their peers than with me: they don't try to pretend they understand something they don't or that they've read something they haven't. The honesty allows more questions to get asked and answered; and for some reason, they seem to be able to help each other understand difficult material better than I can (perhaps I assume too much and skip over necessary stages in the explanation?). When the group has a live question that no one can answer, the assigned reader makes sure it gets directed to me so I can help.

I ask the students to save all of their inkshedding throughout the term; the pieces can either help them study for the exams or find ideas they can explore further for a formal paper. They're required to select what they consider their three best inksheds to resubmit, marked with marginalia from their colleagues, to me at the end of term. I always look at these mini-portfolios of inkshedding when I'm puzzling over a borderline grade.

Exhibit 4.1. Form for Reader's Report

Name: _____   Class: _____   Date: _____   Group: _____

Short titles/authors: _____

Missing responses from: _____

Responses received after report written:_____

Funniest sentence:

Sentence that surprised me the most or pointed out an idea or connection I hadn't thought of:

Weirdest or most puzzling idea:

A question that should be addressed in class discussion:

Sentences (or passages) that confused me or revealed confusion (no need to copy these in full—mark them on the inkshed with brackets and question marks and refer me to that particular student author):

A detailed, helpful summary by:

Interesting reading/writing strategies tried by:

A literary term used as a way into the text by:

Summary/comments/reflections (Inkshedding—feel free to use the back. Nothing you say in this report influences anyone else's grade, only your own—unless, of course, your group has put you in the unfair position of needing to write a report without all responses present.):

Do this report quickly—most of your time should be invested in reading and writing on your colleagues' inksheds. I look through all of them for signs of a real conversation going on in the margins!

Peer Response in Smaller Upper-Level Classes

In classes of twenty-five or fewer students, I'm more apt to use a reading log, requiring each student to do a certain amount of disciplined inkshedding in response to the reading for each class period. At some point during class, if we're sitting around a table or in a circle, we'll pass these logs to the right (or left—the surprise factor can be useful), open to the entry for the day, and take ten to fifteen minutes of class time to read and respond to it, again writing comments or marginalia according to the guidelines above and signing our comments. I ask that students respond to the log of a different person each time so that we've all managed to read each other's work at least once during the term. It's crucial in these smaller classes that I bring my *own* writing and allow a student to read and comment on it while I'm reading and commenting on someone else's.

The discussions following this procedure can be unstoppable: I ask students to share passages that struck them from the reading log they've just read. Though students might have hesitated to advance their own ideas, they never hesitate to display the insights or good questions of their colleagues. Usually, by the time everyone has had a chance to speak, whatever lecture I might have given has been given, embedded in these responses—that is, I'm usually able to take the questions raised and the interpretations ventured and show the students how they make the very points my lecture about the assigned reading would have made. I ask them to take notes during the discussion, and I obviously have to highlight important material for them, provide additional context, and make notes myself of what we have failed to cover so I can mention it next time or at the end of class.

At a few unannounced points during term, I will collect the day's entry at the end of class so I can get a sense of how both the original inkshedding and the commenting is coming along. The students know I will be doing this, but not when; I've discovered that the threat of my collecting their work and the chance that I might, on any particular day, be the reader for their logs, is often all the policing necessary to keep them current with the reading and the writing. Again, they usually want to be part of the conversation. I collect entries at least once early in the term so I can catch students who aren't yet giving substantive comments or engaging with the material in a disciplined, detailed way. Often, all they need is feedback to help them figure out how to get going. At the end of term, they need to mark what they consider their two or three best entries; I collect the complete log to see that all entries are full and present, but I usually read closely only the ones they have marked (more, of course, if I'm puzzling over a borderline grade).

Conclusion: Why I Value Peer Response

I listed earlier the two primary benefits of peer response groups for me—that I can assign more writing than I ever could otherwise and that students learn more from each other, spend more time in each other's heads, than they would otherwise. But other good things happen in both the large lower-level and smaller upper-level classes as a result of these practices:

• I get constant feedback on how the class is going and who is understanding what. I also have lost that killing distrust of students that used to come from the silent moments after I asked what I thought was a good discussion question. I used to think only a few students were doing the reading. Now, I know almost all of them are, and I have access to their written readings at any time. Discussions are substantive and have their own momentum; students talk to each other, not just to me.

• I build my lectures from students' exploratory writing and teach to their questions; and because they know that their questions, their words, and their names might suddenly appear in a lecture, they're more attentive.

• My students begin to lose their assumption that literary interpretation is magic or arbitrary; they begin to see how readers gradually *build* interpretations of texts in public negotiations with other readers—they begin to understand how the wider conversation that is literary criticism works and how they might go about joining that conversation, particularly as they develop the skill of grounding all they say in the text.

• Every piece of their writing gets read and responded to by someone, usually thoughtfully. Further, they do so much exploratory writing that it becomes a resource for studying for exams or for developing paper topics; they come up with ideas worth "growing" into formal essays. Once they have learned the principles of peer response to low stakes writing, they can apply them to higher stakes writing. The peer response groups in my classes also work together to produce a collaborative final exam (but that's a subject for another essay). When I require the students to reread all of their writing at the end of term to select their three best pieces, I don't need to convince them how much they've learned—they can see how far they've come from some of their careless, superficial, or baffled first readings.

• Because they're writing primarily for an audience of peers and writing quickly, students' writing is coherent and lively; there's no tortured prose trying to sound academic or impressive. I learn to look forward to reading student writing, partly because I don't need to grade it but also because it's often funny or thought provoking, full of fresh responses to and questions about material that could otherwise grow stale for me.

• Students make friends. I sometimes forget how lonely college can be for students, especially freshmen, until I come across an inkshedding that says, "This is the only class I have where I get to know and talk to other students—I like that. Otherwise I can go all day without talking to anyone till I get back to my dorm room just before supper." Not always, but often, the groups become supportive mini-communities or mini-families where students feel safe enough to try out and debate new ideas with each other. Occasionally the groups meet as study groups outside of class, especially right before the midterm or final exam. And once or twice, when I've been ill late in the term, the class has held itself for the full period, with groups circulating the inksheds, and everyone reading everyone else's and then discussing the assigned reading for the day. The groups help the students feel they have some ownership in the class.

• Because they're writing about everything they read, my students learn more and remember more of it, much more than they would remember six months later from taking notes on my lectures only. They learn how to use writing to help them learn, to focus their attention, to generate an active heat that makes connections, and simultaneously to record those connections. They learn how keeping a record of their developing thought can actually push their thinking; they're especially convinced of this when they see how the track of their colleagues' thoughts proves valuable to them.

• Finally, students become more fluent as writers—less apt to freeze on an essay exam, more able to write coherently under pressure, more able to marshal supporting detail from the text to advance an argument or develop an interpretation. Many of them, I would argue, become not just more fluent but better writers, which is not surprising. Most of us become better at anything as a result of steady disciplined practice. Yet all of this improvement seems to come about without anyone editing or correcting their writing or pointing to what's wrong with it; instead, readers have usually only pointed to what was intriguing, memorable, or provocative in it. I'm especially grateful that the growth seems to occur without my needing to correct or grade all this informal writing. (Obviously I grade exams or formal papers, but I had always done that before without noticing any particular improvement in student writing over the term.)

Because of space limitations, I have made a lot of assertions here, which it would take a book-length manuscript and many excerpts from student inkshedding to prove—and even then I'm not sure I could "prove" the value of these activities in any conclusive way. As I said at the beginning, many of these practices resulted from necessity; when I first started peer response groups, I felt as if I were trying to leap across a chasm hundreds of feet wide— with hard pointy rocks a mile below. In other words, there seemed wonderful potential for disaster.

Without the terror of the jump, I'm not sure peer response would have worked in my classroom. That is, students aren't good at doing something they have never done before; the first few weeks of teaching them how and modeling the process for them were discouraging. If I'd had the option of going back, I might have taken it, but the ravine looked even deeper from this side, so I stayed where I'd landed and made a go of it. Now, of course, I have the confidence that comes from knowing how the students will be working together after the first three or four difficult weeks, and my confidence and belief carry over to them and make everything easier, less frightening and unfamiliar.

What am I trying to say? That although many forms of writing-to-learn can be tried out in small increments, I'm not sure peer response groups work the same way. They require advance planning, time and energy, and even more, a willingness to exercise enormous amounts of authority up front, restructuring a class and making students take a more active role in their own learning. It may feel so *unlike* learning to them at first that they will resist strenuously. I have occasionally had students drop a course—sometimes A students (who functioned best memorizing lecture notes to give back on exams) and sometimes D students (who realized there was no way they could pass without attending class, reading the texts, and writing about them). I would suggest trying not just a *little* bit of peer response in *all* your classes at once, but trying a whole lot of it, committing yourself to it entirely, in only one class, leaving all your other classes to carry on in traditional ways and make you feel steady and sane while you manage only one risky experiment. Students need a lot of practice to get good at peer response: both they and you will be frustrated if they only do a small amount of it badly.

The only guarantee I'll make is that you won't be bored—and neither will they. And maybe the ravine won't look so deep to you from the far side, and you'll be able—unlike me—to jump back again if you decide a classroom without peer response groups works better for you and your students.

But I'm betting you'll be having too much fun to think about making the return trip.

References

Coe, R. "What Is Inkshedding?" *Inkshed*, Feb. 1993, *11* (3), 1–3.

Craven, M. L. "Inkshed Conferences: Transforming the Conference into a Conversation." *Textual Studies in Canada*, 1995, *6*, 82–87.

Pare, A. "A Response to Rick Coe." *Inkshed*, Feb. 1993, *11* (3), 3–5.

Polanyi, M. *Personal Knowledge*. Chicago: University of Chicago Press, 1958.

Reither, J. "Motivating Writing Differently in a Literary Studies Classroom." In A. Young and T. Fulwiler (eds.), *When Writing Teachers Teach Literature: Bringing Writing to Reading*. Portsmouth, N.H.: Heinemann, 1995.

Reither, J., Hunt, R., and Coe, R. "What Is Inkshedding?" *Inkshed*, Feb. 1994, *12* (3), 1–11.

Sargent Wallace, M. E. "Errors and Expectations; or, How Composition Scholarship Changed the Way I Ask for and Respond to Student Writing." *ADE Bulletin*, Winter 1994, *109*, 23–34.

M. ELIZABETH SARGENT *is associate professor of English and director of the Honors Program at Western Oregon State College in Monmouth.*

*This chapter focuses on assignments that balance personal or
constructive writing and academic or critical writing—an interplay
that is necessary if students are to develop habits of active learning.*

Student Writing in Philosophy:
A Sketch of Five Techniques

Stephen M. Fishman

Changing My View of Writing: Using Writing-to-Learn

My first writing-across-the-curriculum workshop over a decade ago, in 1983,
changed my attitude toward writing.[1] It helped me see that composition could
be used in ways I had previously overlooked, for example, to record impressions, explore texts or problems, argue with myself or develop an internal dialogue. Because the purpose of such composition is exploration, it forced me to
alter my view that writing always came after the research or that one should
always think carefully before one writes. Whereas I used to view writing as the
last step in the process of discovery, I now saw it as an accompaniment of every
stage of discovery. The various *writing-to-discover* techniques I practiced at the
workshop—*freewriting, triple-entry notetaking, response logs*—although only
scaffolding for more polished work, became important elements in my revised
view of the early stages of exploration.

   Not only did I begin to see discovery and writing differently, I also found
that my attitude toward writing was changing. Prior to that first workshop,
writing was painful. When faced with composition tasks, I envisioned my
audience as critical, ready to find fault. And no doubt, throughout my school
and academic life, my audience—teachers and editors—functioned as harsh
evaluators offering scant praise. But because the techniques of writing-to-
discover (or *writing-to-learn*) are directed toward oneself, they invited a less
inhibited way of composing. And writing-to-discover was exciting because it
was a way of digging toward somewhere unknown rather than reporting from
a place already inhabited. Johann Gottfried Herder ([1770] 1968) in the eigh-
teenth century and Benedetto Croce ([1922] 1953) and R. G. Collingwood

(1938) in the twentieth all point to such exploratory work, activity with purpose but without clear-cut destination, as central to creativity.

To be fair to my readers, I acknowledge that there are composition specialists who see writing-to-learn quite differently (Stotsky, 1990; Williams and Colomb, 1990). Such researchers argue that emphasis on writing-to-learn leaves students unprepared for advanced academic tasks. They argue that sophisticated tasks require students to read and research, find focus and theoretical context, and develop appropriate rhetorical strategies prior to the writing stage of their work. Such criticism notwithstanding, I find that introducing students to the often ungraded and informal types of composing associated with writing-to-learn, like freewriting and triple-entry notetaking, helps students become more involved in their learning, helps them attend more closely to the meaning of their writing than to its formal, grammatical qualities.

Changing My View of Teaching: Encouraging Students' Personal Responses

Before sketching five specific ways students write in my classes, I want to mention how my first writing workshop also altered my view of teaching. As I have already noted, writing-to-learn is exciting because it can lead to unexpected places. It is also exciting because it puts a premium on personal response. It wants *my* reaction to a text, issue, or event. It wants to know how *I* generated my reaction and how *I* feel about it. In other words, it asks me to examine what lies behind my response and what may be the consequences. The power of this sort of writing—the energy and passion accompanying it—helped me appreciate what Mary Belenky and her colleagues call "constructed knowing" (Belenky, Clinchy, Goldberger, and Tarule, 1986), that is, the approach to events which asks, What does this mean to me? In other words, In which ways is this text, problem, or story important to me? Constructed knowing stands in contrast to the dominant school or academic way of knowing that Belenky and her colleagues call "separate knowing." This latter mode asks us to step away from texts, stories, and problems to see them more neutrally, to place them in more public contexts.

Recognizing the power of constructed knowing forced me to acknowledge that students need motivation to imitate my ways or the ways of my discipline. I could no longer in good conscience assume that Plato or the free-will controversy would be inherently exciting to students. I realized my assigned texts and I had to share center stage with my students so they could build their own bridges, find their own connections to the subject matter and manners of my field. As much as I want to be their elder guide to my discipline, displaying its ways of speaking and writing, I saw I also had to orchestrate my class so there would be space for students to do their own thinking. I had to help them find their own ways into my field by encouraging them to explore their own reactions to Plato, for example, or to classic philosophic issues.

Although my enthusiasm for writing-to-learn initially led me to focus on its techniques almost exclusively in my courses, now, more than a decade after my first workshop, my classroom goals are more balanced. Rather than emphasizing constructed knowing at the expense of separate knowing, or privileging writing-to-learn over more formal author-evacuated prose, I try to encourage a variety of ways of composing and knowing. I believe that students who move among various approaches to writing (and to the world) develop the multiple perspectives necessary for the learning and change that I seek for them.

Five Types of Writing in My Classroom: Juxtaposing Different Ways of Knowing and Composing

Study Questions. Although I give considerable attention to drafts for term papers and in-class essay exams, the writing that currently takes most of my own and my students' time is responses to what I designate as *study questions*. I assign these questions for each class reading, and they require a mix of straightforward information and personal reflection. As an example, for our reading of Plato's *Crito* this past semester, I asked students to write on these topics:

> (a) *During his trial, Socrates claims he is not fearful of death. Outline three reasons Socrates gives for not fearing death.*
>
> (b) *In the Crito, Socrates responds negatively to Crito's proposal that he flee from prison. Please evaluate these arguments. Is Socrates convincing? If you found yourself in Socrates' position, would you attempt to escape or would you accept the court's decision? Please explain.*

During a typical course, I assign and grade between fifteen to twenty sets of these questions, and presently I let this work count for 35 percent of a student's final grade. Although I spend considerable time responding to these study questions, about five or six hours per week, I find them worthwhile for several reasons. First, they offer me some assurance that students are confronting assigned texts. Second, they give me a clue about my students' ability to understand what for many are new genres employing difficult language and complicated arguments.

In the storm of my initial enthusiasm for writing-to-discover, I became impatient with some of my study questions, ones like "outline three reasons Socrates gives for not fearing death." Answers to such questions suddenly seemed a bit insulting to students, not to mention boring for me to read. After all, it doesn't seem very original to work through a Platonic dialogue by distinguishing arguments, their premises, and conclusions. Further, such questions might be said to demoralize students because I am forcing them to generate answers that are, presumably, already known to me. It would seem that their chances of providing something new to me are slim. Regardless of these thoughts, my experience has been that without such apparently simple information questions, many of my students do not complete reading assignments, do not engage with my discipline's core texts. As important as it is to help students clarify their own reactions to philosophic issues and problems, I believe it's also important for them to experience careful reading, to step into the arguments and mind-sets of people whose language and assumptions are quite different than their own. Besides, I accept that one of my teacherly duties is to show that when, for example, we discuss loyalty to community versus loyalty to principle or family (as Socrates did), it's not enough to be sincere. For students to develop open-mindedness and critical awareness, to challenge their present points of view, they must also learn to situate their beliefs within the conversation about such issues already underway in their culture.

The mix of factual and personal response that is called for by my study questions is significant because it represents the balancing act I try to perform. On the one hand, I want students to speak for themselves, to find their own commitments and points of view. (I add that this is not an easy goal to satisfy, because the majority of my students feel uncertain or indifferent about typical philosophic concerns—issues relating to the nature of God, punishment, freedom, or ethical judgment.) On the other hand, I also want students to learn something about the history of my discipline (their heritage), to become familiar with elements of the philosophic canon. As I work for this balance of personal response and disciplinary rigor, the various forms of writing I employ seem like different characters in a play, my task being to organize their timing, to estimate when one's been on stage long enough and others need their cue.

Classnotes. In addition to study questions, I have had success with a different and ungraded sort of writing that also mixes attention to texts with concern for personal response. My courses usually meet for two one-hour-and-twenty-minute sessions each week. On my current syllabus, I indicate that for each class period there will be a designated note taker. At the start of the following session, this note taker must distribute sufficient copies of her or his summary of the previous day's discussion so that everyone can participate in reading these notes aloud. To get things going, I take notes the first day, but thereafter the designated note taker gets to choose which student will do it next. This way the responsibility circulates throughout the class. The designated note taker also chooses a classmate to begin the class's reading of the notes, and moving clockwise because we sit in a circle, students take turns reading aloud, paragraph-by-paragraph, until the notes are completed.

My classnotes procedure began without much forethought. A few years ago I had a senior engineering student, Andrew Johnston, in my introductory course. (All student names in this chapter are pseudonyms.) Andrew never said much, and when I called on him, he offered only yes and no answers. Despite these minimal responses, I sensed he was intelligent and reflective, and I was frustrated by my inability to increase his participation. I'm not sure why, but one day during class I turned to Andrew who was seated three chairs to my left and said, "Would you mind taking notes today and having copies for every-one next period?" It meant so little to me at the moment that by the time that class period was over, I had forgotten my request. But the following afternoon, Andrew came to my office with a smile and thirty-five copies of classnotes. He had composed them on a word processor in newspaper style, with columns, an editorial, and a cartoon. I was impressed and a little shaken because, although I knew Andrew had potential to be a significant contributor, I had underestimated his ability. Andrew's classmates very much enjoyed his notes, and we kept writing classnotes for the remainder of the semester. Students pre-sented them in different styles, some, for example, as dramatic dialogue, some as baseball play-by-play (a few students striking out and a few hitting safely). The most unusual innovation was made by an older student who got help from his six-year-old daughter. She drew illustrations of justice and injustice as dif-ferent bikini-clad island women.

Most of my students' summaries are less provocative and inventive than was Andrew's. In fact, many are straightforward, almost verbatim accounts of class discussion. As an example, I quote a short excerpt from Brittany Maxwell's notes from spring 1995. Her summary is about class discussion of William Paley, an eighteenth-century British theologian who argues that just as a watch must have a watchmaker, so the world must have a Creator.

Class last Thursday, February 9, got off to a good start as everyone enjoyed Jason's witty notes and his ability to use our new vocabulary word, viz., in a sentence. We were all happy to hear that no study questions were due for the following week.

Fishman then started our discussion by asking how everyone liked the triple-entry notetaking that he had introduced to us. Carrie felt as though it was helpful, and she was able to use it in her education class. Hai, smiling, agreed and found it helpful because you reinforce what you are reading.

Fishman then directs the conversation back to questions that Tricia had on Tues-day about Paley. Like Tricia, Scott didn't understand Paley or his whole argument. Mike Stevens nodded in agreement saying that he was "clueless the whole time."

Rebecca, seeming frustrated, asked Fishman about us discussing the readings before doing the study questions. Fishman explained that it is important for us to work our way through the readings ourselves. He wants us to "experience being puzzled." It was pretty evident from the class discussion that followed that we had all experienced being puzzled while reading Paley.

We then got out our books and Mike Stevens began reading some of Paley's con-fusing words. Evan tells us that Paley is trying to relate the watch to man and how man came into existence.

The reading wears Mike out, so Jake, being a good friend, roommate, and team-mate, continues for him. B. L. expresses her confusion about Paley by saying that she had "no idea, clue, or anything."

We do finally see Paley's point when Mike Stevens tells us that he's trying to say that there is a God. Spence then adds that Paley believes that if you can't explain how things got here then there's no creator, and it's atheism.

Despite the routine character of summaries like Brittany's, I continue the practice for a number of reasons. One, reading classnotes tends to jump-start class by reminding everyone where discussion left off. Two, some students say they pay better attention to class discussion and participate more freely because they know their own notes will be supplemented by an "official" version. Three, I suspect the practice forces students to dignify and pay better attention to their classmates' comments. Note takers tell me they take great care to record everyone's recitations correctly. This sort of mutual respect promotes class community, the sense that what we say is being recorded as part of our common history, the shared stories that help us better understand one another. Four, lots of students get to speak at the start of each class period, if only to read what a classmate said the previous session. There is something communally binding about this part of the practice as well, echoing ritual readings in church or synagogue. And the designated note taker, in adding her or his piece to the textual web being woven by the class, has an opportunity to have the last word on the prior class discussion and set the tone for the next. Five, many students, although initially wary, enjoy the responsibility. For some reason, perhaps because of the large peer audience, students often try to outdo previous note takers, especially if they are their roommates, teammates, or out-of-class friends. Six, in the discussion format I employ, I rarely go to the blackboard to write conclusions or major points. As a result, it's sometimes easy at the end of a session for students to think "nothing happened." Classnotes help remind everyone about the key issues we have discussed and the arguments considered, pro and con, for alternative resolutions.

Triple-Entry Notetaking. In her class summary, Brittany Maxwell mentions my introduction of triple-entry notetaking during a session of my Intro course. She notes that two students, Rebecca and Hai, volunteer that they found the technique helpful. I am unable to report that most of my students make similar claims. To the contrary, many seem indifferent. But because I myself find it extraordinarily useful, I persist. As an example of how I use this technique, I quote from one of my recent handouts:

> *Please do fifteen minutes of "triple-entry" notetaking on pp. 125–130 of Kitto's The Greeks. After completing your notetaking, take five minutes to freewrite a brief essay about this section of the text.*
>
> *Explanation: The "triple-entry" notetaking technique is a way of responding to a text without attempting to memorize or guess what someone else finds important about that work. To do "triple-entry," divide a blank page into three parts. In the right-hand column jot down any sentence or phrase which strikes you (plus the page number where it appears). By "strikes you," I mean a sentence with which you disagree, which you don't understand, which you wholeheartedly endorse, or which triggers an association with something else. In the middle column, opposite the sentence or phrase you've taken from the text, write down whatever occurs to you (in other words, your response). It could simply be—"oh, no." Or—"that's the same point Orwell makes in 1984." Or— "if it's true that I must trust myself, where does that leave science and all its proofs?"*

(In other words, this sort of notetaking is a way of beginning a dialogue with the author of the text.)

Sometimes my chain of response ends with the middle column. But other times I'm lucky and find a response to my response. I record this in the left-hand column. In this third column I might write—"Not only is it in <u>1984</u>, but also in <u>Death of Ivan Ilyich</u>. Ivan, like Socrates and Winston Smith, also tries to follow his inner voice against strong social pressures."

How to generate an essay from "triple-entry" notes? One suggestion involves what is called "looping." Go back or "loop" back through your triple-entry notes and circle anything which surprises or especially interests you. Then look over what you have circled, pick out one phrase to put at the top of a fresh sheet of paper, and begin your short essay.

Whereas most note-taking strategies, like underlining, highlighting, and outlining, are one-way streets, designed to help readers open up and *receive* a text, triple-entry is an interlocking highway. Its intent is to open multiple connections and interactions *between* reader and text. Like student study questions and classnotes, triple-entry is a technique that mixes various modes of thinking and writing. First, it helps students focus on and be critical of a written piece. This might be called triple-entry's separate knowing mode. Second, it also invites students (in the middle column) to attend to their reactions to a piece and (in the left-hand column) to any responses they may have to their reactions. This might be called triple-entry's connected knowing mode. Paradoxically, triple-entry helps a text take on significance because of the way it encourages awareness of reader response (something that at first glance might seem to deflect a reader *away* from a text). Triple-entry thus rests upon what John Dewey called "the double movement in all reflection" ([1910] 1991, p. 79). It rests upon the view that learning involves finding connections, moving back to see the forest and going forward to see the trees. Applied to the study of a written text, it means stepping closer to see what the text can tell me about other things (including myself) and looking at other things to see what they can teach me about the text.

In my philosophy classes, where the abstractness of the assigned reading often leads students to lose interest, triple-entry can help students find ways in which their lives and the written pages intersect. As a result, students sometimes report that whereas more traditional notetaking leads them to forget a text once notetaking is complete, triple-entry, by encouraging the back and forth between their own responses and the text itself, stimulates them to burrow into the reading, to search for more ricochet among text, themselves, and their culture.

Freewriting. At the close of my triple-entry notetaking assignment, I ask students to spend five minutes freewriting a brief essay about a topic or idea generated by that exercise. I want to talk more about freewriting, especially because I put it at the core of writing-to-learn. In its purest form—when the writer begins without any topic in mind—freewriting is primarily a tool of self-discovery. It is a way of finding issues that are tacit or at the edge of conscious awareness. A classic description of freewriting comes from one of the editors of this volume, Peter Elbow.

> The idea is simply to write for ten minutes (later on, perhaps fifteen or twenty). Don't stop for anything. Go quickly without rushing. Never stop to look back, to cross something out, to wonder how to spell something, to wonder what word or thought to use, or to think about what you are doing. If you can't think of a word or a spelling, just use a squiggle or else write, "I can't think of it." Just put down something. The easiest thing is just to put down whatever is in your mind. If you get stuck it's fine to write "I can't think of what to say, I can't think of what to say" as many times as you want; or repeat the last word you wrote over and over again; or anything else. The only requirement is that you *never* stop [1973, p. 3].

I rarely use freewriting in this pure, unalloyed form. However, in my classes, I extensively employ a hybrid called *focused freewriting,* which asks for the nonstop writing Elbow describes but about a specific subject. I often request this sort of freewriting about an issue or text just prior to introducing it in class discussion. I also use focused freewrites to help students develop term paper topics. Of all the writing-to-learn techniques, focused freewriting yielded the most immediate results for my students. I back this claim by offering several reasons.

First, focused freewriting is an effective way to ready students for class discussion. Although in most cases they have responded to study questions, these responses have been prepared outside class, perhaps over a now forgotten weekend. With a just-completed in-class freewrite on their desks, it's a lot easier for students, even the shyer ones, to contribute to class discussion. Second, when faced with term papers, students sometimes give me an "I have nothing to say" reaction. Understandably, they are fearful of graded writing assignments, like term papers. They worry about making mistakes, not being able to discover good topics, not successfully thinking them through. At the least, focused freewriting provides students with a way to get started, an opportunity for them to discover they do have topics they care about. Third, students worry about having too little material. "How long does it have to be?" they ask, hoping my answer will be, "Short." Freewriting is a means of responding to that concern, a way of uncovering relationships, raising new questions, and complexifying topics students fear they have prematurely exhausted. Fourth, most schoolwork is product oriented, focused on external rewards, like grades, that are separable from the process of discovery and composition. Freewriting is a vehicle for developing student self-respect, for helping students appreciate their own ability apart from someone else's evaluation.

For a recent weekend assignment, I asked Intro students to generate term paper topics by writing about any reading they found especially interesting. One student, Rebecca, responded that she had no idea how to start. "Reserve five minutes on Saturday for some freewriting," I suggested. "After you do that, review what you've written, find what's most interesting, and set aside ten minutes on Sunday to write more about it. Also, I'd like to know how you carry out the assignment, so, after you finish, draw a line across your page and describe what happened."

On Monday, Rebecca came to my office and handed me the following paragraphs:

Saturday.

    Yes I will force myself to write on something, anything, or nothing. What struck me while I was reading Walden Two, they were not afraid to do nothing. If somebody in our culture asks what you are doing and the response is, "Nothing," they look at you in contempt. We feel guilty doing nothing. We watch television rather than do nothing. Nothing is an honorable pursuit. Television is for the brain dead.

Sunday.

    The fact that people in Walden Two were content to do nothing impressed me. I suppose "content" is the wrong word. They were unafraid and unashamed. In American society doing nothing is a guilt-ridden activity.

    Doing nothing usually is an activity. It may consist of sleeping, thinking, looking, or listening. These are honorable pursuits, so why do we feel guilty?

    We watch television rather than do nothing. It becomes the central activity to some peoples' lives. Perhaps nothing leads to something and they are afraid of something.

    Rarely do people doing nothing spend all their time at it. Inevitably some idea occurs to them. An idea about which the person needs to do something. Thus nothing is a productive activity.

I started out, Saturday afternoon, at a loss. I forced myself to take my instructor's suggestion and freewrote for five minutes. While doing so the idea about nothing showed up. As I was out at a jazz concert the nothing subject kept bothering me. Sunday morning I woke up and just started writing. Presto, a promising topic.

What pleased me about the result of this assignment was Rebecca's appreciation of a technique for self-starting. Instead of my giving her a theme (or taking away *her* chance to find a theme), freewriting gave her a way to use her own resources for a desired result. Like the other writing techniques I have already discussed—study questions, classnotes, and triple-entry notetaking—focused freewriting combines mixed modes of thought. It is a blend of disciplined thinking and free association, a double movement that juxtaposes narrowing and widening. Insofar as I asked Rebecca to write for five minutes on a class reading that interested her, I was giving her task a focus, encouraging her to be disciplined enough to write with an assigned objective for a designated length of time. Insofar as Rebecca had no idea about a suitable topic or what she would say about it, my freewriting assignment was inviting her to pursue whatever glimmer of light caught her attention. On Sunday, her second day of writing, she used her first piece to help narrow her focus before, once again, using a freewrite to find new connections, new roads to and from "doing nothing." We see her beginning to wonder if doing nothing is misnamed; if, in fact, it is not so much an empty blank as a pregnant pause. She begins moving toward the view that doing nothing is considered dangerous not because it is really a waste of time but because it is often, to the contrary, so productive: a chance to step back and reevaluate present scripts and agendas.

Again, to be fair to my readers, I note that freewriting, like writing-to-discover in general, has its critics. Going back to classical times, Plato, in the *Ion*, ridicules the moments of effective freewriting I have described as "mad." Much more recently, Richard E. Young (1990) disparagingly calls those who connect composition with mystery the "new romantics." Freewriting has also been charged with promoting sloppy habits, ignoring style and grammar, and neglecting careful argumentation. Although I recognize these problems as potentially serious, I remain a freewriting booster. My teaching experience leads me to affirm that like other writing-to-learn techniques, freewriting helps students find personal contexts for their academic work, thereby increasing this work's emotional significance. At the same time, as we see with Rebecca's inquiry about doing nothing, freewriting can also help students turn outward to more public contexts, enriching their work by revealing overlooked assumptions behind a text, attitude, or practice.

Class Response Logs. The final sort of writing I want to discuss is a type of ungraded outside-of-class writing. Once or twice a week, I assign questions about course routines, students' sense of their own performance, or how they believe the course is functioning for them. I request that they answer in a class response log (CRL), which I collect four times a semester. During the opening weeks of class, my questions are usually about their expectations for the course, what must happen for them to consider it a success, and about their obligations to themselves, to me, and to their classmates. Later on, I often use CRLs to learn students' reactions to exam grades, whether or not they were satisfied, and how they might alter their exam preparation to improve. Sometimes, I inquire about their class contributions, whether they feel free to speak their minds or occasionally refrain (and, if so, why). At times, I have asked students which classmates have power in our class, with whom they most and least identify, and whether or not any class discussion has caused them to modify their views.

Unlike the previous four types of writing that I have discussed—study questions, classnotes, triple-entry notetaking, and focused freewriting—class response logs were originally designed to help me rather than my students. Depending upon my concerns during a given semester, I shape the CRL assignment to learn about particular aspects of student experience. The first time I used CRLs, my questions (they usually total fifteen or sixteen) focused on problems that students might encounter when completing assignments. I became interested in the various approaches they took, how their major fields, for example, influenced the ways they approached their written work. In subsequent semesters, I used CRLs to learn about ways community formed or failed to form in my classes. I wanted to see if there were student groups or alignments that stayed steady across the various issues we explored. More recently, I have been interested in classroom authority. I have focused on who gets to speak, who is silenced, and the manner in which gender, race, and class may affect the patterns of classroom discussion.

Although I designed the CRLs to help myself, I also believe they have positive, although indirect, consequences for students. First, CRLs may help students reflect on their own learning, enabling them to develop a residue of information about their best methods for preparing for class and completing assignments. Second, my hunch is that in a modest way CRLs humanize me to my students and vice versa. They bring some of the class "underlife" to the surface, and this helps us see each other more fully. That is, CRLs invite an informal tone, another way for students to communicate with me, a backstage conversation where we acknowledge the wider contexts of student life into which courses must fit. I find it interesting that the class schedule often works so that I read CRLs just before major exams. And each time that happens, I sigh to myself and sense my attitude toward my students becoming more positive. Sometimes, after weeks of studying closed faces, guessing at their silences, wondering what lies behind murky answers to study questions, I feel disappointed and adversarial. But the CRLs give me a chance to see a serious and generous side of my students that other assignments don't normally invite. Almost without exception, students take the CRLs seriously, although I only respond and do not grade them. They answer with surprising detail and length, perhaps because they sense I am seeking information that only they can supply, perhaps because they suspect it's an opportunity for them to switch roles and show care toward me.

Third, in addition to affording students opportunities to reflect on their learning processes and to humanizing student-teacher relations, CRLs give me different perspectives on individual students and on the class. I'm often shocked, for example, by how wrong my impressions have been, how wide of the mark my understanding about why students have responded or failed to respond in certain ways. CRLs have revealed that certain class discussions, which I took to be routine, actually made some students seethe and "bite their tongues." At other times, when I have asked someone, "Have you anything else you'd like to add?" and I have accepted their no as a straightforward answer, the CRLs have shown that no masked more than I knew. The logs indicate that sometimes it actually was a declaration of silence, the beginning of withdrawal in response to what a student perceived as a hurtful put-down by a classmate. I close this section by offering brief excerpts from two typical and recent CRL entries by Kyle and Mike, both participants in the William Paley discussion summarized in Brittany's classnotes reported above.

The CRL question Kyle and Mike are answering is: "Do you feel you have adequately stood up for your values/positions/ideas in class discussion? Please give an example where you were satisfied with the position you made clear to your classmates."

Part of Kyle's response was as follows:

I was satisfied with my points when we were discussing Paley. The class was having trouble with one of his passages and I was able to somewhat decipher it. A couple of classmates said my statement helped them. This made me feel good. It's good to know that your statements aren't scrutinized by your classmates. This makes speaking in the future easier.

Mike wrote:

I don't feel as though I've made a significant contribution to the class as of yet, but I will. I don't think I have because I don't think I've said anything clever enough to make someone pause for a moment and say, "Wow, that's a really neat way of looking at this," or "that's a really good insight." I guess I haven't really done that because I'm usually trying to figure out what the readings were about myself, no less be able to give valuable insight. If I could understand the readings better I think I would contribute more. Reading is not my forte.

These CRL entries illustrate that even brief glimpses of students' perspectives can be helpful. My own impression of Kyle was that at this stage of the class his contributions had been meager. But from his own standpoint, it turns out he was quite satisfied with his contributions and, especially, with the class's response to his comments about Paley. Mike Stevens, in contrast, surprised me with his critical self-evaluation. Contrary to his own view, I had been rating his class participation quite high. Neither CRL, of course, gives me a clear idea about how best to help these students, but these CRLs do give me additional details about Kyle and Mike, items and background that increase my chances of more effectively understanding and responding to these students during the remainder of the semester.

Conclusion

The five types of writing I have discussed are not the only written work I ask of my students. I also require term papers, drafts for those papers, and in-class essay exams. I have singled out these five types because I believe they're less common than those I have chosen not to discuss. Further, four of the five I have singled out require very little instructor time. Freewriting, classnotes, triple-entry notetaking, and class response logs are all ungraded, and although I collect the CRLs, my responses to them are brief, mostly marginal comments. Yet all these, in my view, heighten student thinking and involvement. Freewriting and triple-entry notetaking are especially helpful at increasing my classroom repertoire. They offer different ways to construct class discussion. I can ask students to read from their freewrites. I can divide them into small groups to share their triple-entry notes or the brief essays they have written based on them. These strategies add variation to the rhythm of my classes and, I believe, help foster student participation. In addition, both freewriting and triple-entry notetaking allow me to write along with my students, and risking sentimentality, I admit I'm always gratified when I look up from my own desk to see students busy at theirs. There's something binding, a chance for mutual respect, when we work simultaneously at the same tasks, grapple with the same issues or texts, risk equally as we reach without guarantee for something to say.

Of the writing assignments I have sketched, study questions require the most time. I grade them; they are lengthy, and I feel obliged to provide detailed responses. Are they worth the time? For me, the answer is yes. Study questions help me decide how students are doing, which ones are making a consistent effort, which adjustments in reading and writing assignments I should consider for the future. It troubles me that some students complain loudly (in their CRLs) that the study questions are too demanding, but I can also report that others say they are not bothered by the effort and mention they look down on friends who drop the class because of the high workload or who make marginal efforts to just slip by.

Despite my continuing affirmations about the writing in my classes, there are moments I wonder why I continue. There are times I think enviously about colleagues who are successful with short-answer questions, identification matchups, and the three-paragraph précis. What keeps me to my present course is that first workshop when I experienced writing differently, when I found it exciting and realized I could use it to hear myself out, bring forward fresh perspectives, venture into problems whose parameters are unclear. Ultimately, the reason I continue is that I want my students to have that same experience.

Note

1. The workshop was held under the auspices of the University of North Carolina-Charlotte Writing Project, an affiliate of the National Writing Project, and led by Sam Watson and Leon Gatlin, to whom I will always be grateful.

References

Belenky, M. F., Clinchy, B. M., Goldberger, N. R., and Tarule, J. M. *Women's Ways of Knowing.* New York: Basic Books, 1986.

Collingwood, R. G. *Principles of Art.* Oxford, England: Oxford University Press, 1938.

Croce, B. *Aesthetic: A Science of Expression and General Linguistic.* New York: Noonday Press, 1953. (Originally published 1922.)

Dewey, J. *How We Think.* Amherst, N.Y.: Prometheus Books, 1991. (Originally published 1910.)

Elbow, P. *Writing Without Teachers.* Oxford, England: Oxford University Press, 1973.

Herder, J. G. *On the Origins of Language.* (A. Gode, trans.) Chicago: University of Chicago Press, 1968. (Originally published 1770.)

Plato. *Ion.* In *Great Dialogues of Plato.* (W.H.D. Rouse, trans.) New York: Mentor Books, 1956.

Stotsky, S. "On Planning and Writing Plans—Or Beware of Borrowed Theories!" *College Composition and Communication,* 1990, *41,* 37–57.

Williams, J., and Colomb, G. "The University of Chicago." In T. Fulwiler and A. Young (eds.), *Programs That Work: Models and Methods for Writing Across the Curriculum.* Portsmouth, N.H.: Boynton/Cook, 1990.

Young, R. E. "Arts, Crafts, Gifts, and Knacks: Some Disharmonies in the New Rhetoric." *Visible Language,* 1990, *14,* 341–350.

STEPHEN M. FISHMAN *teaches philosophy at the University of North Carolina at Charlotte.*

This chapter presents advice on developing inquiry-based writing projects, consulting with students throughout their work on a project, and responding in ways that are respectful and instructive.

Developing and Responding to Major Writing Projects

Anne J. Herrington

I really put distillation together when I wrote that lab.

It restructured the way I thought about things.

I kind of like the way she lets us discover the story instead of telling us outright "This is what it is." . . . A major thing is what questions are you left with. That's a good way to go about interpreting.

She somehow conveys the impression that she has high expectations. It's almost intimidating, but she's not intimidating as a person. So, you do that higher-level work for her.

In my research studies of writing in various disciplines, I have been fortunate to interview many students and hear many comments like these pointing to the potential that writing activities—both longer, formal writing projects and briefer, informal projects—can offer for learning. I have learned as well, from other students and other classroom situations, that this learning potential cannot be taken for granted. Further, I have learned that we teachers, as the ones who develop those activities for our students, are central to determining whether and how that learning potential will be realized. In this chapter, I will be guided by the assumption that developing writing activities, consulting with students as they work on a major writing project, and responding are important vehicles for the kind of teaching that fosters engaged, inquiry-based learning. I will focus primarily on longer, more polished writing projects (what

Elbow terms *high stakes writing*), instead of the equally valuable shorter and more informal writing activities (*low stakes writing*).

Developing Writing Projects

In Chapters Two, Three, and Five, respectively, Toby Fulwiler, Art Young, and Stephen Fishman present valuable suggestions for low stakes writing activities that encourage engaged, inquiry-directed learning. Building on their suggestions, I want to focus on three central principles that apply as well to higher stakes writing projects:

Make them inquiry or issue based.
Keep them focused, but open enough for students to develop their own angle or interest.
Offer guidance for going about the inquiry and writing.

Make Writing Projects Inquiry or Issue-Based. Writing activities that invite inquiry or speculation, or pose a problem or intellectual puzzle are more likely to invite thinking—extending one's knowledge, formulating a new understanding for oneself, changing what one previously thought—than are rote recall tasks, or what one student called "spitback" assignments. When one student said she "really put distillation together when I wrote that lab," she was speaking of the learning value of a laboratory report in a chemical engineering course that posed for her the intellectual challenge of explaining in words what she had previously understood only through equations. The act of *writing* the report—especially the discussion section—forced her to connect the equations and textbook explanations with what she had observed during the lab, going beyond vague and disparate thoughts to formulating a more integrated and precise self-understanding. In a different way, when another student said, "it restructured the way I thought about things," he was commenting on how an inquiry-based writing project to find out more about another culture by interviewing two people from that culture in conjunction with reading a book had given him an entirely new perspective on that culture. That restructuring—a profound change in thinking—was fostered both by the interviewing that invited empathic knowing and by the writing that asked him to make some meaning of what he had heard and read. For both of these students, the writing they did was much more than just a rote exercise to demonstrate their knowledge.

For some projects—especially in advanced courses—the intellectual challenge may be readily apparent; in others, it may not be. For instance, you may want to use writing as a way for students to work out their understanding of a basic theory or various scholars' positions on a topic—something about which you have already worked out your own understanding. For example, from my research, I find that students in introductory courses are often asked to compare and contrast particular scholars' views on a given subject. In the worst case situation, the assignment is given; students write their essays; the teacher corrects them. One student succinctly described the limited purpose such an assignment served in one class, "He just wants to see whether we did the reading." Another commented on the experience of doing a similar assignment in another class, "It was repetitive and boring." And it was probably repetitive and boring for the teacher as well. One way to make such projects more interesting and challenging for the student—and ultimately for you—is to build a focusing question or problem into the assignment. For instance, for a comparison-contrast task, you might ask students to write a *briefing paper*, interpreting a specific situation from each scholar's perspective and then, say in a sociology class, evaluating the implications of these different perspectives for formulating social policy. The resulting briefing papers might then serve as the springboard for a class discussion of the scholars' positions.

Equally important as posing a challenge in the assignment itself is conveying through your manner that you value original thinking and questioning, not simple regurgitation of readings or your views. In the chemical engineering lab, for instance, the students perceived that their professor wanted them to do more than just say *what* happened; as one student explained, "AJ wants to know *why* things happen." Bringing students' writing projects—their ongoing work and the substance of their final drafts—into class meetings also reinforces the value of their intellectual work (see Chapter Three).

Another strategy for creating intellectually challenging writing projects is to build in an audience and purpose. For example, a colleague of mine in physics has posed this assignment to his students in a junior-level class:

> *Write an essay explaining to a freshman Physics 141 student why an airplane flies. Assume that the student has seen the Bernoulli equation in this course and now wants to know why it works. Emphasize physical (qualitative) arguments—on the molecular scale. [The assignment concludes with a couple of questions to prompt thinking.]* [Mullin, 1989, p. 343.]

For the students, this task presents a genuine intellectual challenge because the answer is not immediately apparent: "solving" the problem requires them to grapple with their understanding of the equation as well as use it to explain a physical phenomenon and move from quantitative to qualitative thinking, a skill that is important for these students in physics.

Keep Writing Projects Focused, but Open Enough for Students to Develop Their Own Angle or Interest. This physics task is clearly focused on a specific intellectual challenge. Although it is not open in the sense of inviting students to choose their own topic, it is open in that it invites original thinking, because students didn't have an available textbook or lecture explanation to draw upon. The task also invited original thinking on students' part in deciding how to present their response to this new audience (the freshman Physics 141 student). This kind of question also increases the likelihood that the professor will have more varied, original, and thus potentially interesting essays to read than if he had just asked for an explanation of the Bernoulli equation.

More obviously, the openness may be present by giving students latitude in choice of subject. For instance, in an introduction to anthropology course, a colleague of mine asks students to interview an older person and write a life history focusing on "how that person has experienced his/her working life and how he/she has perceived and been affected by aspects of inequality in the workplace" (Herrington, 1992, pp. 247–248). In this instance, the assignment poses a general inquiry-based question, specifying the focus while giving students some latitude to define it further for themselves and select the person each would interview.

Offer Guidance for Going About the Inquiry/Problem Solving and Writing. For the anthropological interview project, the professor, Sylvia Forman (Herrington, 1992), gave students guidance and included in-class workshop time for developing interview questions, conducting interviews, interpreting the interview notes, and composing a draft. In presenting the assignment, the professor also made clear her evaluation criteria, specifying that students were "not only to trace one person's development, but to use the example of that person's experiences and reflections on them to understand features of the larger social system."

Evaluation criteria that include the intellectual demands of a project—not only the formal writing qualities—can serve to guide students as they work on the project and you as you give them feedback both in process and at the conclusion of the project. In other words, these criteria can serve as formative guides, not simply summative assessment guides (Odell, 1992). For example, for a research project in an upper-level environmental economics course, a colleague, Donald Tobey, specifies criteria not only about project scope (length, minimum number and type of sources) and presentation (for example, organized, clear, well edited, accurate citation of sources) but also about the research approach: "Be analytical in your approach using concepts read and discussed in the course. . . . Use concepts accurately and precisely. . . . The focus on your analysis should be primarily *economic*, rather than technical or scientific" (Herrington, 1992, p. 246). He also builds in occasions for coaching students in their research and analysis as they work on the project.

Coaching and Consultation Throughout the Project

The time between my initiating a writing project and students' completing it is when I feel I can do my most fruitful teaching because my students are actively engaged in a challenging project that their peers and I can assist them on. Our role is to serve as consultants, leaving each student in charge of her or his project. I try to fill this role by building in periodic occasions for consultation, each of which begins with the student assessing where she is with the project and indicating any questions she has of consultants. Here's an example from a short research essay project I assigned in my first-year writing class. I

ion. To begin, I ask each student to
she or he wants to explore, what she
nts to find out, and what feedback she
. I present this initial plan as a way to
lp identify what they want to inquire
est. I do not ask for an outline at this
e kind of edited and organized listing
ain points) an outline calls for is sim-
It presumes you know where you're
e plans, and then I offer brief coming to possibilities.

Bibliography. Midway through the project, I ask for a brief memo stating again the focus of the project, the key sources with a brief assessment of each in relation to the writer's project, next steps, and any questions or concerns students would like to consult on. Typically, we discuss these in a private conference, although I could instead easily and quickly respond in writing. (I got the idea for these progress memos from two chemical engineering professors who ask students to write weekly progress memos as they work on extended process design projects.)

Draft with Cover Note. For all drafts, I always ask students to write a brief cover note or letter for their peer respondents and me, indicating what they're most satisfied with, what they're still working on or having difficulties with, and what they would like feedback on. Last semester, one student who was investigating Native American religions commented in a cover note:

> I am happy with the way this paper came together but I am concerned about the infor-
> mation I provided on both sides of the spectrum. Which ways do you think I should
> elaborate? Maybe my point was to get away from organized religion. Do you think if
> I incorporate this idea it will make the essay more sound?

She received feedback from two peers, each writing a full page letter of response. Here are excerpts from both (all student names are pseudonyms):

> Dear Mary Anne, I like that you've explained why you went out to search for a new
> religion. I like your sense of exploring. I think that your paper definitely shows that you
> have made a choice. . . . Because you say that the Catholic experience was "not prof-
> itable," maybe you should say more about why NA faiths are profitable for you. What
> do you get from them? . . . John

> Mary Anne, Your main purpose was to show why you believe the Native American reli-
> gions are right for you and why Christianity is not. Your development looks OK. You
> mentioned that you took the "lessons" you had learned from the Catholic church with

you when you went "fishing." I think that might be an important thing to elaborate on.
Catholicism can't be all bad if you've learned some basic values from it. . . . Celine

I thought John and Celine had responded to Mary Anne's own concerns well and posed some productive questions to her. As a consequence, I wrote a shorter, half-page response. Here's part of it:

Dear Mary Anne, Good start! This will be an interesting essay. Helpful peer responses.
I felt like your main point did come across. . . . [Then I indicated one place where she
alluded to the role of nature in NA religions where I wanted to hear more.] Anne

Final Draft with Cover Note. For this cover note, I ask students to indicate what they're most satisfied with, what they learned about writing and research in doing the project, and what feedback they would like from me. Here's an excerpt from Mary Anne's cover note:

Once I nailed down my topic the paper just started to roll. I was able to find in my
research things that could support my ideas as well as extend my knowledge. I defi-
nitely dominated this research paper and that was something new. The peer editing
and your review of the midprocess draft were very helpful. I could clearly see a differ-
ence when I cleared up the parts that were confusing to the reader. I would like you to
address my use of the research. Should I have included more quotes? Is there enough
information included and is it worthwhile? . . . I also learned that it is much easier to
do the paper in steps rather than the night before it is due! Mary Anne

In my final response to Mary Anne, I indicated my overall positive evaluation of the essay, framing my comments in relation to key criteria we had developed for the essay, and responded to her questions. All final drafts were also "published," so the full class could read and respond. Such publication is another way of validating students' work and bringing their viewpoints and ways of writing into the classroom.

In citing this chain of exchanges, I hope I have conveyed how it's possible and fruitful to create an ongoing conversation about a work in progress, one that encourages students to keep assessing their own work and soliciting feedback that they think will assist them, one that allows for a teacher and *peers* to offer formative feedback along the way. (See also Chapter Four.)

Although such in-process consultation may seem time consuming, it is not. Actually, I have found I can reallocate my time, making briefer comments on the final drafts than I used to in order to make these in-process comments. Also, peers share the responsibility of offering feedback, and I believe that is instructive for them. The benefits make it worth it. Being able to participate in a constructive way during the process of inquiry is much more satisfying than offering only after-the-fact comments. Most importantly, I have found that students find these in-process comments more helpful than final draft comments because the in-process comments related to a project students were still working on.

The same is true for my former colleague, Donald Tobey, the economics professor from whom I got the idea of asking for an initial plan. The first step for the research project in his environmental economics course is for students to complete a *topic sheet* containing "a paragraph or two indicating the importance of the topic and the general analytical approach you plan to use" (Herrington, 1992, p. 246). For Tobey, this explanation gives him an opportunity to advise students early on in their research—to see whether they have a workable issue, advise them in reshaping it if necessary, and make suggestions on how to proceed. For instance, one student proposed to investigate the economic feasibility and environmental impact of refining oil shale for energy. After explaining her idea, she commented, "If this argument does not cover 15 pages I could also include the debate on who will mine shale since most of it is on public lands." Here's Tobey's response:

> *Kim, Sound topic. Go to it!*
>
> *Oh, I don't think you'll have any problem covering 15 pages! Mix of "feasible" question (incl. estimated costs & prices, of other sources) and impact should be a sound one, raising such questions as:*
>
> *—Incidence & types of Ben. & Costs*
> *—Assumed demand shifts for energy + related goods and services*
> *—Alternative measures to protect environment, & their impact on producer, consumer, etc.*
>
> *While you may not find an abundance of sources specifically aimed at econ. of oil shale development, there should be some (including articles in something like Fortune or Business Week, maybe?). Broadly you'll want to apply economic sources to this specific issue. You might check with Cindy B. about sharing a couple of "background" sources I loaned her on oil shale* [Herrington, 1992, p. 249].

As this response illustrates, Tobey used his response to comment on the appropriateness of the issue, propose major questions to consider, and suggest sources. His response also reads like a comment in an ongoing conversation, picking up on her comment and continuing in a manner conveying his personal presence and his encouragement.

Responding. Tobey's response to his student's topic sheet illustrates traits of an effective response. It is

Addressed as a response to the writer. It's important to remember that when we're responding, we're responding to a person, not correcting a paper. When I begin a response by addressing the person by name, it helps me remember that focus on the writer.

Responsive to the writer's concerns and questions. Note that Tobey picks up on Kim's concern that her topic may not be broad enough for a fifteen-page paper.

Constructive in tone and substance.

Points to what is done well.

Makes specific, descriptive comments, giving the person an idea of what should or could be done next. Note that Tobey names the traits of her main question that make it workable—essentially restating key criteria from the assignment—and names some possible subquestions she might pursue.

Focused.

Resists taking over the project.

These same traits are evident in a response made to a second draft of a research essay for an anthropology course. In this instance, the teacher, Sylvia Forman, felt the draft was not reflective of a student's capabilities and that it still needed a good deal of revision: note that students had already written first drafts, received feedback from peers, and revised (Forman and others, 1990; Herrington and Cadman, 1991.):

> Sherri, Your main point in this paper is an important one, and you've located key critiques to go with the two major sources. You do not make much of all this material: in particular, you do not effectively incorporate the criticism of Turnbull and Holmberg and you don't draw out T's & H's inferences about the implications of their studies. . . . The number & variety of typos, grammatical errors, & misspellings is extreme. I have marked only a small portion of them. In sum, this reads as a very rough draft of a potentially interesting paper. Sylvia [Herrington, 1992, p. 255].

Forman addresses the student by name and signs the response with her own name. The response is also firm, yet still constructive in tone, particularly in the closing sentence, "a very rough draft of a potentially interesting paper." In the opening sentence, Forman points to what is well done and then goes on to note in specific terms what is missing and, by implication, what needs to be done to strengthen the paper. Note also Forman's remark about grammatical and typographical errors: "The number . . . is extreme. I have marked only a small portion of them." She resists becoming copyeditor for her students, which really serves no purpose for learning. Instead, she marks obvious errors in an excerpt of the paper and then names the kinds she sees. In short, she offers guidance but leaves the editing work to the student.

When Forman received the third draft of Sherri's paper, she again addressed her comments to Sherri and again aimed to be instructive by offering specific descriptive statements about the draft, one that Forman still felt was far from satisfactory:

> Sherri, This is an improvement over the previous draft. You make better use of your sources. Overall, the organization is more logical. The more limited use of quotation is appropriate.
>
> The number of technical writing errors, and of typos, is still excessive. . . .
>
> My major concern with the paper, at this stage, has to do with your reliance on repeated general assertions, instead of direct movement toward a conclusion using spe-

cific facts/points. Contrast the paragraphs I've commented on at the top of p. 3 and the middle of p. 5 [both overly general] with the paragraph on the Minn. experiment at the end of p. 5 ["This paragraph is an example of using specific information to build toward a conclusion"]. . . . Do you see the significance of the distinction? . . . Sylvia
[Herrington, 1992, p. 256]

Note that to show Sherri what she means by her point about "a direct movement toward a conclusion using specific facts/points," Forman points to a passage where Sherri has done that well, contrasting it with one where she has not. (See also Elbow, 1993, where he notes that positive reinforcement is more conducive to learning than negative reinforcement.) Note also that in Forman's course, students had the option to revise again before submitting their portfolios at the end of the semester—most did, including Sherri—so that the professor's comments were more likely to be considered.

Conclusion

I have quoted fairly extensively from both students and teachers because it is in their voices that we hear the kind of inquiry, reflection, and coaching that we should be trying to achieve in our own classrooms. We can cultivate that environment by approaching our students respecting their capabilities, challenging them in intellectually engaging ways, coaching and nudging them to that next higher-level work that each is capable of, and conveying our interest in them and what we learn from them.

References

Elbow, P. "Ranking, Evaluating, and Liking: Sorting out Three Forms of Judgment." *College English*, 1993, *55*, 187–206.
Forman, S., Harding, J. A., Herrington, A. J., Moran, C., and Mullin, W. J. "The Junior Year Writing Program at the University of Massachusetts at Amherst." In T. Fulwiler and A. Young (eds.), *Programs That Work: Models and Methods for Writing Across the Curriculum.* Portsmouth, N.H.: Boynton/Cook, 1990.
Herrington, A. J. "Assignment and Response: Teaching with Writing Across the Disciplines." In S. Witte, N. Nakadate, and R. Cherry (eds.), *A Rhetoric of Doing: Essays on Written Discourse in Honor of James L. Kinneavy.* Carbondale: Southern Illinois University Press, 1992.
Herrington, A. J., and Cadman, D. "Peer Review and Revising in an Anthropology Course." *College Composition and Communication,* 1991, *42,* 184–199.
Mullin, W. "Writing in Physics." *The Physics Teacher,* May 1989, 342–347.
Odell, L. "Context-Specific Ways of Knowing and the Evaluation of Writing." In A. Herrington and C. Moran (eds.), *Writing, Teaching, and Learning in the Disciplines.* New York: Modern Language Association, 1992.
Tobey, D. M. "Writing Instruction in Economics Courses: Experimentation Across the Disciplines." *Journal of the Northeastern Agricultural Council,* 1979, *8* (2), 159–164.

ANNE J. HERRINGTON is professor of English and director of the writing program at the University of Massachusetts, Amherst, and coeditor (with Charles Moran) of Writing, Teaching, and Learning in the Disciplines.

This chapter suggests ways teachers can respond to what they observe in their students' writing so that students can understand, respond to, and learn from their teachers' written comments.

Negotiating the Margins: Some Principles for Responding to Our Students' Writing, Some Strategies for Helping Students Read Our Comments

Elizabeth Hodges

> *What I want most when a teacher responds to my writing is address the content. What do I present effectively or ineffectively. And why effective or ineffective. In order to help me I need any teacher to move beyond grammatical issues. To me it almost serves as a copout to only write comments on students' papers like tense problems, rough, awk. Well, what does that mean?*
> —Iris P. Bodiford

I have been collecting data on response for six years now in a series of projects using *talk-aloud protocols* as interview instruments (Hodges, 1992, 1994). From teachers who have worked with me, I have gathered *response protocols;* the teachers respond to their students' essays aloud as they generate their written responses in margins and end spaces, getting as much of what they are thinking on tape as possible. I get to hear their readings and rereadings of students' papers. I hear their conceptualizing and then their writing of comments. I hear their thoughts on students' abilities and performances. And almost always, I hear crucial conversations teachers try to have with their students, but more often than not, and most unnecessarily, these are conversations that their students never engage or become engaged in.

From their students, I have collected *reading protocols.* We meet. I return their essays. We talk some—about writing in general, about their class, about the essay before us—and then the students read their essays aloud, incorporating and responding to teachers' comments as they go. I transcribe these tapes and make copies of the essays with teachers' written responses. Students who go on to rework essays bring me copies of their revisions. Thus I have been able to get a bit more than a glimpse of what goes on behind teachers' written commentary, that actual commentary that students see, as well as students' impressions of their essays and their teachers' written thoughts about the essays. To examine the data, I look at places where the teacher has initiated conversation in margins and end comments, and then I compare what's written to what teachers said on tape. These points of initiation I then pair with students' corresponding responses.

This strategy for analyzing the relationship of teachers' response to students' reception of that response has given me a rich sense of teachers' goals for the content and rhetoric of their responses. I have been able to see what does and does not make it into the margins and end comments, what correlations exist between the teachers' responses to individual writers and their essays' content and the teachers' abilities to develop clear goals for responding. I can see when teachers and students are having or not having the same conversations and can characterize the two sides of such conversations. I can identify patterns in both teachers' and students' modes of response.

This research has led me to some critical conclusions. The margins of students' written work are the ideal site for teacher-student conversations about what and how students are thinking about their essay subjects, about how teachers respond to their thinking, and about the subjects themselves. Regardless of which discipline we teach in, we can do some of our most successful teaching in the margins and end spaces of students' written work, perhaps more than we can in any other site. The margins allow us to work one-on-one with our students and to leave a record of what work we have done that students can return to repeatedly. However, what I see most often in the margins are conversations that misfire. I see teachers fail, in myriad ways, to articulate what they observe in their students' work so that their students can understand and respond. I see students ignore important messages in our feedback, sometimes because teachers have framed these messages so that they seem idiosyncratic, matters of personal choice. I have seen students get angry and shut down, not just in terms of particular essays but in terms of the entire semester's course.

In brief, written feedback fails more often than not, largely for reasons that are avoidable. In the first section of this chapter, I offer three teacher-student interactions that let us eavesdrop on the teachers' voices behind their written responses and on the students' voices negotiating these written responses. Each case suggests some principles for our own response practices, for successful response practices. Each case also emphasizes that though most teachers can improve on their practices, a key to making written commentary work is teaching our students how to make sense of what we say and then how to do what they need to do.

Case 1: Terry and Ms. Thorn

There is a world-weary, even cosmic shrug I have seen students give, many times, when I have prompted them to explore the relationship of their teachers' comments to grades or requests for revisions. The following is from a transcript of a conversation I had with one such student, a participant in a 1993 data collection:

"Terry, how do you go about fitting what Ms. Thorn has written in your margins into your own essay?" I ask.

"I'm not all that up on comments," he responds.

"What do you mean 'not all that up on comments?'"

"I mean they don't mean much to me most of the time. Sometimes I don't bother reading."

"Hmmm. Do you have any sense of what responses you want teachers to make to your writing?" I ask.

"I really don't because it just, it just baffles me anyway how I can write a paper on something I don't care about at the last possible minute and rush it in thinking it's trash and I get back 'Good' and a B or A. I mean why?"

"So you do have a sense of what you want. Explanation of what a grade or comment means, to begin with?"

"Yeah. I yeah. Explanation would help."

"How does the end comment explain your grade here?" I ask.

Terry turns to the end of his paper and laughs, a short bark of a laugh. "'Good' and C C is that a C minus?" I look and say yes. "She writes," he says, and then he reads, "'Good. Your paper is basically well written but I need you to further develop certain parts of it and I need one more text. See my notes and see me if you have questions. I'm looking forward to your revision.'" Terry laughs, "So do I. Look forward to my revision I mean."

I ask Terry what he is going to do now about making revisions. He shrugs and asks what I suggest. I suggest that he go back through the essay, reading it, and make note of where she asks for more information, "further development," I clarify. "That makes sense," Terry responds and writes down "where she asks for more," a note to himself. Then he asks what she means by "I need one more text." I know the answer; the assignment asked students to synthesize three texts from her list, and he used two from that list and another not on the list. But I think he needs to work this out with Ms. Thorn, so I suggest he first go back to the assignment and see if he missed something. If he still can't figure it out, I suggest he ask her. "That makes sense," he says again. Finally, I ask him how he might find out what Ms. Thorn means by "Good" in her end comment. He shrugs.

"Ask her, Terry. Ask her," I say. He is noncommittal. I wonder what, if any, of these commonsense strategies he will take up in an effort to understand his teacher's comments and improve his essay. I wonder if and when he will learn how to be an active participant in the conversations teachers have with him in the margins of his writing and in their end comments.

Beyond noncommunication, what else is wrong with this picture? My first thought when I look at the transcript excerpt is that Terry, though clearly intelligent and thoughtful, seems to have no clue as to how to find answers to his very reasonable questions about his teacher's comments. If, indeed, that is the case, Terry and his like need to learn to initiate these crucial interactions with us. They need to learn that they can seek us out to talk about their work, that we expect them to. So perhaps one of our tasks as responders to students' written work is to teach students to approach us and learn to ask questions about their work. That is one way to help them learn to learn actively. I think making clear to them that we are accessible involves relatively simple moves on our part. We can return their written work with time still left in class for them to read through our comments and ask questions then and there. We can teach them how to read our comments by modeling the different ways we might read a piece of their writing.

We can make sure, too, that they believe us when we invite them to come see us. Ms. Thorn's invitation, "See my notes and see me if you have questions," at first may seem a fair offer, but not when I have read it on a trillion other essays. I suspect that by the time our undergraduates are juniors and seniors, they have seen the same invitation a few times themselves. Such a comment appears near the end of almost every end note, and its very phrasing is distancing. "See my notes" comes before "see me," and the conditional "if" can really silence students who know they have questions but are not sure what those questions are and how to ask them.

Enter the cosmic shrug. We can, as responders to their writing, help students learn what the questions are simply by explaining our comments more—perhaps by offering models in our comments for how to structure statements, use certain terms, articulate certain kinds of concepts, order statements leading from cause to reaction. In their response protocols, I hear teachers often anticipate questions a comment might evoke. Those who are more successful in their responses are the teachers who anticipate and frame such a question here or there in the margins. For example, Ms. Thorn could have said, "I need you to use one more text. Why? Remember the list I gave the class? You only used two, not three, as I required." At that point, Terry might ask, "But Ms. Thorn, I used a third text which fit better with my discussion. Wasn't that text a good choice?" And if he takes that question to her, negotiation and conversation are alive and well.

My second thought when I look at the excerpt is that I know more about Ms. Thorn's responses than Terry does. Ms. Thorn has, as part of my study, responded to his essay aloud, taping her thinking and generating of comments as she goes. She tells me, *not* Terry, that he's "got a natural flair for using English. His papers start out with a lot of grammatical problems, but he's got a real ability to focus and a really dynamic way of structuring crucial sentences so that he really nails what he wants to say. He can catch most the problems if he proofreads." To Terry, she describes his paper as "basically well written." My immediate question is obvious: isn't it more important for Terry to hear these positive responses than me? If he knew what she thinks about his writing, wouldn't he be able to move closer to some knowledge of himself as a writer, to ask her what she means by "a natural flair" and so on? Perhaps at some point she will voice her praise to him, but why didn't she do so in her end comment?

My third thought about the story of Terry and Ms. Thorn leads me into the grist of this chapter. When we respond in writing to what our students write in response to our assignments, we are responding to and conversing with individual learners. We can probably do more teaching in the margins and end comments of essays than we can in any lecture or conference. We can help students learn to think in our subject areas. Response is one-on-one. We can see which students need what kinds of help and either offer that help or guide them to it.

Responding to students' writing is itself an act of writing. As such, we who respond must be as concerned with issues of structure, clarity, focus, purpose, and voice as we want writers in any discipline to be. We need to write well in the margins and end comments, and by *well* I do not mean spelling and correctness. I mean clear, connected, useful, respectful comments that guide students to see their written representations of their thinking so that they can become both better thinkers and writers in all areas of the work and study.

Case 2: John and Ms. Byrd

In an essay on discrimination toward men, John wrote about images of men in home product commercials and movies that involved men in chores traditionally allotted to women. When he receives his essay from Ms. Byrd, he reads through the essay jerkily, pausing where Ms. Byrd has written comments, generally without making comments himself. Often when he reads Ms. Byrd's comments aloud, he misreads in some minor ways that in reality make a tremendous difference in meaning. For example, John reads his own sentence, "Besides the male being discriminated against, I feel that there is one additional party suffering. The manufacturers." Ms. Byrd has circled "suffering," which John takes to indicate a misspelling, but Ms. Byrd has written two questions in the margin, "So men are suffering because of commercials?" For her, this is a question. John reads it as a statement, ignoring the question mark, comments, "Yep," and goes on to read the second question, this time hearing the question mark. "Does this make sense?" he reads, voice rising at the end. "Nope," he answers, and goes on.

While generating this question during her reading of his essay, Ms. Byrd had said, "This is a good point, I think, but I need him to understand that he hasn't really explained this suffering, the way they are suffering." She then writes, "So men are suffering because of commercials? Does that make sense?" Ms. Byrd goes on to say that John needs to "focus on making the connection between commercials, society, and self-image." Knowing that this is her central response theme, I can read her margin and end space questions much more productively than can John. For me, these comments all ask this writer to push further into his content and then to make and articulate necessary connections. For John, when he reads the questions as questions, each stands alone. In Ms. Byrd's end comment, he finds and responds to a series of questions with simple non- or going-nowhere responses. Ms. Byrd has written, "John, why did you want to write this paper?"

John does not respond.

She then asked, "Have you personally ever felt insulted or embarrassed by a TV commercial?"

John responds, "No."

Ms. Byrd continued, "Do you *really* think anyone pays attention to commercials?"

John responds, "Yeah yeah yeah I think people do pay attention to commercials."

She then asked, "If you do, why don't you write as much in your paper?"

John does not respond, and he offers no further response to the rest of the end comment until he realizes he's received a C. The C makes him angry, and he crumples his essay into a ball and says, "I thought a B would be more appropriate. I thought I did a pretty good job. That's my personal opinion."

The distance between John's reception of his teacher's responses and the goals of her responses is tremendous. In her reading protocol responding to his essay, her major comments focus admirably on a specific core goal with John as a writer. She wanted John to see the need to examine and articulate his premises and to make connections between his assertions and those premises. For John, because her responses are single moments, each response flying solo, teacher and student fail to connect. No progress is made.

Sadly, there existed a simple strategy for avoiding this problem. Happily, we can learn from this, their failure to communicate. We often have a major theme or so underlying our responses. We simply must make those themes overt. We can, with little effort and major payoffs, guide students in how to read our comments. For example, what if Ms. Byrd had written across the top of John's first page, "John—As you read through your essay, I want you to note that all of my questions are asking you to work on one important aspect of writing: make connections between your assertions about commercials and self-image and the relationship of that connection to societal values." Had Ms. Byrd announced her theme at some point in her comments—across the top of page one, at the start of the end comment, perhaps even in a response cover page returned with the essay—her questions and comments would have more easily cohered as a single, ongoing comment. And had she penned in one specific example, modeling for him how to make those connections, John might have come to a realization about a writing principle that he would carry with him into his other writing.[1]

Case 3: Rob and Ms. Elliott

Rob reacts at great length to two seemingly simple questions Ms. Elliott asks because he does not understand, as a writer, what she is asking about and why.

Her questions rely on a certain response from Rob; they assume that his linguistic awareness needs only a nudge to be in tune with hers. So twice she prompts him, rather than asking him directly and specifically, to write sentences that structurally complete two incomplete comparisons in his essay. Rob's essay tells of his surprise visit to a friend on St. Croix. His main point is that the openness and trusting nature of the people he met there led him to return to the States with a new way of approaching people. Relating an anecdote in which Rob and his friend knock on a stranger's door near midnight, in need of a hairbrush, Rob has written, "Jim [the stranger] seemed a little different to us at first, but he soon 'took the cake' when he invited us in for drinks." To this single sentence, Ms. Elliott has responded, "How different?" and "From whom?"[2]

During the response protocol she taped for me, Ms. Elliott talked about her primary goals with Rob as a writer—to help him strive for greater accuracy in his use of language and to help him recognize when he needs to expand on his ideas.

Frustrated because he thinks Ms. Elliott does not understand what he is saying, Rob wrestles with her seemingly simple questions for a little over ten minutes, coming up with quite a few ways to read and answer the questions "How different?" and "From whom?"[3] I finally stop Rob and explain that there is a writing principle she wants him to see. I expand her comment: "Who is Jim different from? In writing, we are supposed to name both parts of any comparison we make, so 'Jim was so different from any stranger I'd expect to answer his door near midnight in Richmond.'"

It takes only that much for Rob to understand *what* Ms. Elliott is asking for. He goes on to struggle with *why* she is asking, why that principle for writing. He points out, rightly, that the story comes after a lot of narrative that as far as Rob is concerned, clearly contextualizes Jim's response to their knock. He argues that his writing group understood without his stating his comparison overtly because they have the same urban background Rob brings to his St. Croix adventure. They understand about strangers knocking on doors for bizarre reasons late at night. I prompt him, "But what if they didn't share your knowledge and experience? How would that door be answered in Richmond?" Rob responds, "With a semiautomatic." We laugh, but when I say that he just answered the question, "How different?" Rob grows serious and launches into disparaging self-evaluations of his inabilities as a writer being products of his behaviors as a speaker. He says, "I think it's just one of those examples like you don't write the way you talk okay? That's a little thing I was told a long time ago. Maybe I just don't ah maybe I don't speak correctly."

In truth, I don't think of Rob as lacking oral fluency in the communities he has most travelled in, but I think he does nail the nature or realm of his writing problem exactly. In a nonacademic oral recounting of this incident, or even in a personal letter, an overt comparison would probably come across as superfluous, redundant, following as it would a sequence of briefer anecdotes that demonstrate a clear difference between the behavior of people Rob is meeting on St. Croix and that of people in his urban home. But as a developing academic writer, he needs to obey rules of given/new information and make some statement to this effect: "Opening the door and greeting two strangers with a smile, Jim seemed a little different at first from what I would have expected back in Richmond. But the extent of that difference became clear when he invited us in for drinks."

Toward the end of his rereading of his essay and his teacher's comments, Rob returns to these two questions because Ms. Elliott's end comment has addressed Rob's need to see where he does and does not need to include explanation. As he talks to me, Rob begins looking for reliable rules for when and when not to expand: "So I mean for every fact do you have to have an explanation for it or just can't you take it for granted? I mean this [explanation] is something that maybe should have been and I'm not saying it can't be but in my paper I don't feel like I should've 'cause I did think about that about saying more about that and how well I thought I should explain and before she said that I had too much explanation 'cause I ran her through everything I did."

Rob's reading of his teacher's comments and his essay reveal much that could have helped Ms. Elliott understand more about his needs as a developing academic writer and thinker, his knowledge about using language, and his potential as a writer. Indeed, his responses remind us of the bridges many students need to span between their oral fluency and their academic writing.

Learning to Read Students and Teaching Students to Read Us

To students, our ways of reading their written work are mysterious. Students tend to attribute this mystery to subjectivity, and though they are occasionally right, though we must monitor our personal and idiosyncratic notions of what are reasonable and unreasonable responses, there are other more complex reasons for variances in our ways of reading. We vary in contexts so far as where we teach and the discursive practices of our disciplines. We vary in our backgrounds as writers and readers so far as how we *think* we were taught to write, how we actually *learned* to write, how extensively we have written, and how we feel about ourselves as writers. We vary in our own strengths as writers, in our abilities to make articulate and useful observations to students about their writing. We vary in our beliefs about what good writing is as well as in our beliefs about just where students should be in their literacy development when they reach us—as freshmen or seniors, majors in or electors of our courses. Our students feel our variances to be problematic. Our students are right. In many ways, it is fine, even important, for us to vary as audiences for their texts, but we must be willing to explain how we read our students' work and let our students help us become better readers of their work. We must learn to be candid about our practices, and we must develop practices that teach students how to engage in reading our responses. For example:

Demonstrate how we read students' work. One strategy I have found most successful in my own classes and in those taught by teachers and graduate students I work with is to model how we read a student's response to an assignment by reading a text aloud and commenting as we go—pausing to answer questions we evoke, to explain comments our students don't understand.

Write with our students. When we give an assignment, we sometimes write our own responses and share our own struggles with our classes, letting them see us in action, drafting and revising—letting them respond to *our* writing.

Take time to hear students' responses to our comments. When we hand back writing we have responded to, we leave time in class for students to read through our comments with us there to help them, and we encourage students to write responses to our responses.

Take time to help students incorporate our responses. Sometimes we devote an entire class, even two, to students' work with our responses, with us moving from student to student as he or she reads, questions, responds to us, begins to revise.

In a very real sense, the best response always addresses content and presentation of content above all and always speaks to the writer in terms of revision. In my work with writers at any level, inexperienced to artisans, when we come to the end of a semester, we talk still of "what next?" During any semester, my students learn to write rich *writers' memos* (Sommers, 1989), cover letters for their essays in which they tell me about the piece they are handing in. At the end of a semester, they write a final letter in which they reflect on their work for the semester, commenting on the changes they see in themselves as writers as well as upon the growth they see in their written work. But most importantly, they talk about what they will continue to work on—not particular written work, but writing concepts they have yet to fully grasp. In my final letter to them, I similarly review their work and their growth, and I similarly talk to them about directions to go in, concepts to think about.

Our students usually enter our postsecondary classrooms fluent in their oral arenas, fluent readers of texts that reflect their interests, but more rarely fluent as writers. They need, simply, lots of practice writing (and reading and speaking) and a lot more practice than they have had, to this point, being read by real readers who are out to communicate, not correct (Geisler, 1994). We need to read their work as we would expect a colleague who is also an ally and a support to read our work—honest and critical, yes, but in terms of what works as much as what does not, and always in terms of that next draft.[4]

When we respond as real and complete readers, we engage students in written commentary that goes both ways. When we read students' work only as teachers, we tend to read it as in some other galaxy than our own and our colleagues' and thus are less likely to engage students in any sort of conversation—mostly, we will deliver monologues, soliloquies, sermons, lectures. Real readers engage in content, laugh, groan, and ideally do not start out looking for trouble. Really good readers are sensitive to writers' uses of language. We hear it; we can examine it and see how it works or does not work; we engage in conversations with writers that involve all facets of the writing. And if we take those skills and read our students' work as we would "real writing," then we have much more to say that helps our students grow as writers and learners. Writing is, after all, a rich mode of learning.

Principles into Strategies

In the context of response to individual pieces of writing, successful comments are both local (those comments that target a specific statement, passage, or point in a text) as well as global (those comments that give overviews of a text and that give cohesion to local comments). Academic writing is analytical. It is, from start to finish, a writer's thinking on paper, often thinking in action. It is a conversation between writer and reader. Thus, as readers, we must speak first and foremost to content—first offering our responses to the subject matter and the writer's ideas, then offering our responses to the writer's written representation of the subject matter and his or her ideas. General readers, those who are not responsible to the writer in any way, may not see or have a need to separate content and presentation thereof. They can read solely for information. If they dislike the subject or its presentation, they can turn the page. But as readers who are teachers, we have responsibilities to the writer and thus need to read more consciously and in a variety of roles (Straub, 1996). We must always invoke the general reader in us because that reader, be it an employer or an editor, in the end is the litmus test of a writer's success. But first, even foremost, we must read as teachers, guides, and coaches and read with an eye to how our students' presentations of their subjects aid or thwart their goals with potential readers.

Conclusion: Margin and End Comments Guide

A clear relationship between margin and end comments is crucial. Students need to be able to incorporate margin comments meaningfully as they read their returned essays. Margin comments need to lead like trail markers to the end comments. There may be several trails for a student to follow—say, one focusing on structure, a second on providing the thinking behind claims, a third addressing problems with word choice. But the student must be able to follow the comments and this means that what we put into the margins must be direct and complete. This means, too, that end comments, whether accompanied by grades or not, work best when they tell students the stories of how we read their essays, how we see the whole of a piece working, where reading is smoothest and why, where we run into trouble, get tripped up, and why, and finally what transformation(s) might move the piece closer to its goals. Margin and end comments connect our readings to students' texts, connect us to our students, and thus help students reconnect with what they have written so they can return to it with some distance. When comments don't make these connections, we give students no directions to go in.

Some of the best end comments tell the story of how we read our students' pieces of writing, with emphasis placed on the most important part(s) our stories. For example, the writer of the following end comment addressed two aspects of an essay that stood out as the points where the essay author, Charlene, might best reenter to revise. These problem spots were not the only problem spots, but when Charlene addressed them successfully, other problems disappeared, distinguishing for the teacher where Charlene needed yet to focus.

Charlene—When I finished your three paragraphs, I felt like I was well into an essay focusing on your love of maps like the kind I keep in my glove compartment. I have a real attraction to those sorts of maps, myself, so I was probably disposed to seeing "maps" and making that connection. So I was surprised when your focus shifted, in paragraph four, to psychological maps. As I read further and understood that your initial discussion of maps intends to set up road maps as an analogy, I went back to the start to see if I got tripped up again. I did. You need to indicate, at least for this reader, earlier—perhaps in a paragraph you will add, perhaps in a title that says more than "Maps," the expanded definition of maps that you will be working with. In other words, there's a chasm between paragraphs three and four that you must bridge.

Now, when I try to follow the argument you begin on page 3, I do fine until page 5, paragraph 2, when you propose "mapping" as a solution to family arguments. You don't show me how that would work, so as a reader, my immediate response is "interesting, but what do you mean in practice." But the idea intrigued me and I found myself puttering in the kitchen thinking about ways to use your concept of mapping to solve tensions in my household. So I am willing to believe you, but I think you need to give some examples. You refer earlier to a breech that has existed between your sister and the rest of the family. You generate a map of how you see her thinking to work. Could you generate a map, perhaps, of how you see the relationship among you, her and your mother to work and speculate as to how mapping that relationship might help solve some of its problems? You don't have to use that example, of course, but doing so would offer the reader a "tight package," a chance to travel through the same "territory" from different perspectives.

I cannot offer a step-by-step guide for responding. In fact, such guides, examples—from our own experiences as students, from our colleagues' practices—however well-intentioned will probably fail us. We need to be the readers we are and respond with the principles I have addressed here in mind. Let me close with some thoughts from a few of the many who have taught me the most about responding to writing.

Sometimes I don't express designs [goals? intentions?] explicitly, and I just like to know what's going through your mind as you read or finish the piece. If anything strikes you—an aside, for instance—note it on the page. And anecdote, a reference. These kinds of immediate responses are not necessarily academic, but they give me clues as to how I am affecting my audience.
—Chris Kopczynski

Short of telling me what to say and exactly how to say it, responses should guide my work. I provide the ideas, sentence structure, grammatical choices, even many other choices. The teacher response then should, ideally, recognize or realize my goals and

voice and assist me in bettering what is already written. I'm not saying a teacher isn't entitled to his or her opinions about my style, and I would want a teacher to make that clear, point that out. I always assume a teacher has more experience in the entire writing process than I, and I look for this experience-based wisdom to appear in comments on papers. I look for a fresh perspective in responses. Writing is overwhelming if I can't step away from it and see it. A teacher's responses can help me do that. I look for that.
—Carrie Beeton

I think that the teacher must remember that the student is a person and has feelings even if they have only basic skills, and that what the teacher says will be taken to heart—even by students who "don't care."
—Sheryl Hosey

Notes

1. When I write "come to a realization," I am actually thinking and wanting to write "had an epiphany" or a "bingo moment," as one of my students has called such moments of sudden clarity and understanding when knowledge, however tacit, becomes yours to control. Learning to write is mostly a matter of discovering and grasping concepts, not rules. We learn through practice, in leaps and bounds and stumbles, just like we learn, perhaps intuit or feel suddenly, the logic behind mathematical formulae or the physical principles for how to carry through with a racket or fully extend a swim stroke.

2. In her defense, I want to note that Ms. Elliott also commented on Rob's odd use of "took the cake," a problem that Rob identified as "hearing the term so much you don't think about what it means."

3. That Ms. Elliott *does* understand what Rob is saying is clear in her response protocol, but for whatever reasons, throughout her written comments, she does refrain from letting him know she understands. There are few easier ways to get students to stop listening.

4. I think in part I have learned to be a good responder to my students' work by suffering bad responses from readers I have sought out for my own work. My least favorite reader pounces on typos as errors and quibbles about insignificant problems, an awkward sentence, dust on top of a door, never talking to *me* about what *I* am saying and how I am saying it. My favorite readers assume typos are typos, perhaps mark them, which I appreciate, but they *engage* me in conversations about what I have said. We learn from each other about writing, about reading our own writing, about reading each other's writing. I am fortunate. Nowadays I have four good readers I can count on. My students and my readers' students are fortunate because we have learned to read them as we do each other.

References

Geisler, C. "Literacy and Expertise in the Academy." *Language and Learning Across the Disciplines*, 1994, *1* (1), 35–57.

Hodges, E. "The Unheard Voices of Our Responses to Students' Writing." *Journal of Teaching Writing*, 1992, *11* (2), 203–218.

Hodges, E. "Some Realities of Revision: What Our Students Don't or Won't Understand." *English in Texas*, 1994, *25* (4), 13–16.

Sommers, J. "The Writer's Memo: Collaboration, Response, and Development." In C. M. Anson (ed.), *Writing and Response: Theory, Practice, and Research.* Urbana, Ill.: National Council of Teachers of English, 1989.

Straub, R. "Teacher Response as Conversation: More than Casual Talk. An Exploration." *Rhetoric Review*, 1996, *14* (2), 374–398.

Elizabeth Hodges is associate professor of English at Virginia Commonwealth University and codirector of the undergraduate writing program and co-coordinator of the M.A. degree concentration in writing and rhetoric.

*In this presentation of basic guidelines for responding to student
writing, the central thesis is that teachers' comments should reflect
their instructional goals for individual students. Fewer, and more
carefully designed, comments are likely to be more effective than a
large number of unfocused responses.*

When Less Is More: Principles for Responding in the Disciplines

Ronald F. Lunsford

If one wants to know how best to respond to student writing, it would seem
good to ask experts on composition theory what they do. That is what my colleague Richard Straub and I did several years ago. Our recently published text,
12 Readers Reading: Responding to College Student Writing (1995), reports our
findings. We began our study by sending our twelve readers[1] fifteen samples
of student writing, complete with background information on the courses in
which the writing was produced and the writing abilities (and experiences) of
the student writers.[2] We then asked the readers to respond to these writers as
they would if they were members of classes the readers were teaching.[3] Once
we collected these responses, we devised a rubric that allowed us to analyze
the data we had collected.

Our first impulse was to determine the ways in which these readers'
responses differed from one another. As we worked with our data, however, it
became more and more clear that there were certain basic similarities in these
readers' responses. In chapter five of our study, we listed and discussed the following seven principles for response that evolved from our study:

1. Our readers write well-developed and text-specific comments.
2. They focus their comments on global, not local, concerns.
3. They frame most of their comments in nonauthoritative modes of commentary.
4. Their responses are carefully thought out and purposeful.
5. They are designed to help students approach writing as a process.
6. They are mindful of the rhetorical situation for the writing.
7. They are adapted to the student writer behind the text.

We sorted the seven principles into four key categories of teacher responses: Development and Specificity, Purposeful Commenting, Correctness, and Extra-Textual Response. Within these categories I shall explain briefly what is meant by each principle and then discuss the ways in which all seven seem applicable to responding to writing in the disciplines.

Development and Specificity

Our first principle deals with the length and language of teacher comments (principle 1: our readers write well-developed and text-specific comments). Unlike the teachers in our study, many teachers write undeveloped, cryptic comments such as those in the following list. These comments appear in the margins of student texts, often without any clear indication as to what words, phrases, or sentences are being referred to.

Undeveloped Comments
vague
do we?
tense!
tone?
all people?
good use of quote

Although the comments in the next list are certainly not long, they make specific references to elements in the texts, and they set up a conversational model for the interaction between teacher and student.

Developed Comments
What's your main point here? If it's that you disagree, put that idea up front and explain.
You have given us a summary of the article. Why? You can give your view.
Are you implying here that time for prayer would give protection? If you're not saying that, then how is a reader intended to take this sentence?

Of course, it takes time to write such conversational comments as these. If one has a large stack of papers before him, it is one thing to go through and write one-word responses (such as "good," "vague," "tone," "style") in the margins; it is quite another to talk with the students about what the reader sees (and doesn't see), understands (and doesn't understand), in the text. One might argue that there simply isn't enough time for these conversations. The teachers in our study were mindful of this problem, as illustrated in the subsequent discussion.

Purposeful Commenting

As I think about the principle represented in this section (principle 4: our readers' responses are carefully thought out and purposeful), I am reminded of an anecdote told by a colleague of mine, Sam Watson. He often recounts the story of his first year or two of teaching, years in which he would approach each student text with the aim of pointing out every possible problem in the text. However, the long hours of marking and the comment-littered papers did not produce the results he was aiming for: in fact, they seemed to produce no change whatsoever in student writing. In reflecting on those days, Sam says, "I was trying so hard to be sure that the students would learn to write better, and they seemed to be trying equally hard not to." Fortunately for his students (and for his own sanity), Sam soon came to the conclusion that in some cases "less is more." The twelve readers in our study seem to agree. They average just over three issues per paper marked. That is not to say that they mark only three items in a paper, but that they arrive at a set of themes for their responses. If they have decided that a student needs to work on transitions, they may mark two or three examples of problems with transitions, and make one reasonably fully developed comment (either in the margin near one example of a poor transition or in the end note). This comment might be two or three sentences long, allowing the teacher to give the student a mini-lesson on the issue, rather than some vague notation (such as "transition") that merely serves to put the student on notice that he has a problem of some sort.

This principle is one of the most important in characterizing the twelve readers in our study. In looking at papers marked by many teachers (both writing teachers and teachers in other disciplines), I often get a picture of a marker-of-errors hovering over the text, looking for some trigger to set off an alarm and cause him to attack a passage in the paper. In contrast, when I think of the readers in our study, I have the image of relaxed and reflective readers, who sit back in their chairs to take in the whole of a student's paper before deciding on a strategy for teaching some important principles, and who then carefully construct a set of comments designed to carry out that instruction.

Correctness

The readers in our study attend to what the students are saying rather than to the way they are saying it (principle 2: our readers focus their comments on global, not local concerns). In our analysis, we placed responses into three large categories: matters of form (such as spelling and punctuation, word choice, and sentence structure), matters of content (such as organization and ideas), and matters that reach beyond the text itself (such as the student's personal experience and writing process). Only 21 percent of our teachers' comments dealt with formal issues; 55 percent of their responses concerned content. (The other 24 percent were dedicated to extra-textual matters, which I shall discuss later.)

Interestingly enough, given the reputations of writing teachers, only 6 percent of their comments dealt with issues of correctness (spelling, punctuation, and other mechanical matters). One might argue that these numbers would be partly controlled by the characteristics of the writing, that writing with few errors would allow teachers to attend to content. However, the fact that only

13 percent of the errors that could have been noted were actually referred to in these teachers' comments makes it clear that they were choosing, very consciously, not to devote a great deal of time to error.

When asked what they like about responses they receive from teachers in the disciplines, students often say that these teachers "don't care how you say it, they just want to be sure you know what you are talking about." Teachers of writing and teachers in the disciplines, themselves, have bristled at such comments as these and have argued that students will not value writing until everyone in the university takes writing seriously. Nothing in our study would undermine such a claim. However, it is clear that for our teachers, writing is much more than correctness. The same should be true for teachers in the disciplines. If we attend to errors or to the form of our students' writing, rather than responding to what they have to say, we may well cause students to want to write less. Because most of us get better at those things that we care enough about to practice, the result of such attention to issues of form and mechanics may well be the opposite of what we would want.

Extra-Textual Response

As noted earlier, 24 percent of the comments made to student writers in our study dealt with matters outside the narrow confines of the text (principle 5: our readers' responses are designed to help students approach writing as a process; principle 6: our readers are mindful of the rhetorical situation for the writing; principle 7: our readers' responses are adapted to the student writer behind the text). These comments may deal with such matters as the following:

Writing Process

Did you try any prewriting activities to help you develop your paper? I have the sense that you are limiting yourself to a narrow set of examples here.

Student's Personal Experiences

Do you wear seatbelts when you drive? Have you known someone who was injured as a result of wearing his or her belt?

Rhetorical Situation

What do you think your readers will know about this issue [of prayer in the schools]? What will be your major obstacle in getting them to see things from your point of view?

Classroom Situation

John made a comment about your paper the other day that I thought was very perceptive. He was troubled by the fact that he couldn't decide exactly what you saw as the climax to your story.

Writing Assignment

Your paper is certainly interesting, but I don't think it fits the requirement that you "explain" a concept to your readers.

What can we make of such responding practices? Simply put, they suggest that the teachers in our study believe that in order to achieve their ultimate goal of helping students become better writers, they must move beyond the confines of student texts. This is not to suggest that they do not attend to those texts; certainly, much can be learned by a careful examination of textual matters. But if students are to improve their overall writing abilities, they must reflect on the ways in which they produce texts, the various factors that help and hinder them in different writing situations.

Surely there are analogies in the other disciplines. Obviously, the primary goal of a science teacher will be to assist students in learning science. Because the processes by which students learn are inextricably bound to their personal backgrounds and knowledge, it seems logical that teachers' responses to scientific texts might profitably go beyond the actual information in the texts to deal with issues of process and student knowledge. A student who consistently misunderstands certain concepts in evolutionary theory may well be, consciously or unconsciously, fighting against scientific theories that do not fit into his worldview. Teachers who limit their commentary to what is in the text will lose the opportunity to elicit information that could prove helpful to both teacher and student. For example, how might one respond to a student who presents such misinformation as this:

> Although Darwin claims that humans came from monkeys (and our textbook agrees with him), this theory just won't wash. There are far too many missing links for this theory to be believed. And after all, it is really just a theory, not the truth.

The teacher can attend to the text in some of the following ways:

> This isn't what Darwin says.
> The textbook doesn't accept Darwin's original theories.
> No one thinks that Darwin's theory, in its original formulation, is still valid.
> The fact that there are missing links does not, in and of itself, invalidate a theory.
> Theories, by definition, are neither true or false. They are more, or less, valid, depending upon the evidence that can be offered in support of them.

But how could a teacher who wants to get beyond the impasse represented by the language in this text respond to this student? I suggest that such questions as the following offer a useful alternative:

> Where does Darwin make this claim? Could you find the exact passage and then critique it in light of modern evolutionary theory? Do you find these modern statements objectionable also?
> You are implying a kind of chain of being from monkeys (apes) to humans? Can you draw the chain as you think Darwin meant to represent it? What sources (Darwin's own writing or writing about him by others) has helped shape your picture?
> Can you give me an example of a theory that you accept as true? What convinces you of its truth?

What do those who take an evolutionary point of view have to say about these missing links? Why do you find their position less than convincing?

The first set of text-based responses to this student's assertions about Darwin and evolution point out the inaccuracies in the text. The second set ask the student to do some thinking that may, at least, give the teacher some insight into how the student has arrived at this inaccurate statement. With luck, the questions could help the student begin to do the kind of thinking that may result in his learning something about science in general and evolutionary theory in particular.

Issues of Control

Finally, the twelve teachers in our study can be characterized as nonauthoritarian in their approach to student texts (principle 3: our readers frame most of their comments in nonauthoritative modes of commentary). This is a rather complicated concept and would require considerable discussion were I to attempt to get at the subtle distinctions made in our book. For my purposes here, it is probably enough to say that these teachers do not take the steering wheel out of the students' hands. This is a metaphor that a good friend of mine uses when he teaches me principles of computing. In our sessions, he is generally patient, standing over my shoulder telling me what keys to strike, and when, and thereby helping me learn to do for myself. However, occasionally, I will get myself into a situation that is going to be very hard for him to get me out of from his guiding position, and he will say, "Here, move over, and let me drive a minute." A few quick strokes later, he will have things working and will return the keyboard (or steering wheel, in terms of his metaphor) to me.

I suspect most writing teachers find it very easy to identify with this metaphor. When the student writes a sentence such as "When I have pressure or a deadline, I know I have to do my paper right now, and I have to be concentrated," the natural response is to say move over, let me drive (see Exhibit 8.1). This is clearly the most economical response to such a sentence. The teacher knows how this sentence should be written, and any indirect comments that ask the student to cast about looking for the right answer only serve to draw attention to the artificiality of the writing situation. As a result, many writing teachers have moved further and further away from making comments on structuring issues such as this, except in what they call *editing sessions*—sessions in which they model how sentences may be revised. But in other situations, they accept the fact that learning writers will produce sentences that are not as elegant as those written by more polished writers. They reason that if writers produce more sentences, their sentences will get better. And they suspect that writers who have many of their sentences rewritten for them will feel less inclined to produce sentences.

As I have discussed, the teachers in our study devote less time to issues of correctness, wording, and sentence structure than to matters of content. In one sense, then, this tendency to focus on matters of content is a move away from control. Responses to content, however, can themselves vary significantly in the degree of control they exercise. Our twelve teachers strive not to be overly controlling in their responses to content issues. It is easy to fall victim to the temptation to take control of the student's ideas, with such controlling comments as the following:

Poor sentence structure. [Negative evaluation.]
Put the conclusion in a separate paragraph. [Imperative.]
What about starting with this point? [Advice.]

There are other less controlling ways to comment, as the following examples illustrate:

This word seems just right. [Praise.]
How old were you? Were you in the 7th grade? 10th? [Closed heuristic question.[4]]
How do you distinguish between morals and prejudices? [Open heuristic question.]
First, you say that the law is a violation of a person's freedom. [Interpretive.[5]]
As I read your essay, Steve, I felt as if I were there with you, motoring along I-75, imagining Lake Ivanhoe in increasing detail as first one and then another fishing hole floated past my window. [Reader experience.[6]]

One might ask whether, given the teacher's responsibility to guide student writing, she should avoid all controlling comments. Clearly, she should not. However, she should be careful not to couch too many of her comments in controlling modes. The teachers in our study used both controlling and noncontrolling comments, but they were careful not to be overly controlling, as shown by the fact that they framed only 29 percent of their comments in what we call authoritative comments with the rest in some form of less controlling commentary.

Again, there are similar strategies that teachers in the disciplines can use. Before moving to them, let me acknowledge that we all use writing for various purposes, among them, testing how much (or what) students have learned. In a writing assignment designed to test, response doesn't seem terribly complicated: the student determines how well she did on the basis of a grade. If there is a comment, it tends to be a justification for or an explanation of the marks given.

However, teachers in the disciplines often give writing assignments designed to encourage students to think and learn about a subject in the process of writing about that subject. In such a situation, it doesn't seem appropriate to limit ourselves to the same kind of "right" and "wrong" responses we might use in marking a writing test. The more the teacher can open up the process by asking questions, telling the student how he is reading her work, or even giving personal reflections on what the student is saying, the more the student will be encouraged to think about what she has said.

In reflecting upon how our comments can open up, and shut down, student learning, it is important to differentiate between various types of questions we can ask. It makes a great deal of difference whether the teacher is asking a question that has a definite and clear-cut answer (closed heuristic question) or one that asks the student to reflect on a concept that doesn't lend itself to absolute answers (open heuristic question). It might be argued that it is the teacher's role to know the answers to the questions he asks, because he is, in fact, the teacher. Certainly, there is validity to this point of view. But to the degree that his goal is to interest the student in becoming a learner in a particular discipline (as opposed to a memorizer of certain facts about the discipline), the teacher must find ways to elicit the kind of writing that allows him to respond as a fellow inquirer, rather than the repository of all knowledge in this field. (For examples of controlling and noncontrolling responses to scientific writing, see the previous responses to the student writing about Darwin. On the one hand, those responses that are text based tend to be controlling, to close down discussion by making absolutist evaluations of texts—that is, they tell the student that what he has said is incorrect. The responses that go beyond the text, on the other hand, tend to be questions, many of which the teacher doesn't have answers for. They open up inquiry rather than closing it down. It is no coincidence, by the way, that these two phenomena—textual versus extra-textual and authoritative versus nonauthoritative responses—complement one another. As the teacher focuses on the text, he tends to narrow and confine the student. As he moves beyond the text, he opens up possibilities.)

Caveat

In beginning this essay, I noted that when Rick Straub and I began the study that led to the writing of *12 Readers Reading,* we first focused on differences among the teachers' responding styles. At the risk of seeming to undermine what I have said above, I would like to mention briefly some of the differences we found. There were dramatic and obvious ones. For example, we found, very much to our surprise, that six of the readers made few, or no, comments in the margins of student papers. The other six ranged up to a high of 66 percent marginal (as opposed to end) comments. We found that some of those who made marginal comments wrote very neatly in the margins of student texts, and others wrote within the student's text, or in some cases corrected the student's text. Some teachers used very dark ink and wrote in a bold hand; others wrote in light pencil marks and, in one case, wrote in such small print that one almost needs a magnifying glass to read what she is saying. (Interestingly enough, none of the teachers used red ink for writing on student texts.)

As I have said, on the whole, the teachers in our study avoided authoritarian responses. However, there is a wide range in the degree to which they guide (or control) student writing. That range is reflected in the responses two teachers made to a student text entitled "Street Gangs: One Point of View." (See Exhibits 8.1 and 8.2 for sample passages from the two teachers' responses.) Once one gets past the obvious differences in the way the comments look and the places in (and on) the text that the teachers choose to write, there are some very real differences in the control the two teachers wish to exert. Edward White, whom we label the most controlling reader in our group, makes several corrections on the student's text, rewriting the end of one sentence and telling the student how to begin another sentence. He implies a negative evaluation in one case ("This sentence makes us expect something else"), and he praises the student's detail in another—before implying a negative evaluation: "we need more even here." With the exception of an implied audience in his use of "we" and "us" (in some comments not shown in this sample), all of White's comments refer to issues in the student's text.

Anne Gere makes no corrections on the text; in fact all of her comments are written neatly in the margins of the student's paper. In the sample shown here, she writes six sentences, five of which are questions. Within these questions, she moves beyond the text to suggest that the student draw experiences from his life and consider the effect his writing will have on his reader. Although several of her questions imply there are ways to improve the text, she makes no evaluative statements.

The significant differences in the responding styles of these two teachers are captured in the summary comments we make in *12 Readers Reading*. In our overview of his style, we say of White: "Edward White is a close critical reader. It seems he goes to the text looking for, and in his comments is able to put his finger on, what he sees as the key problems that need to be worked out in the writing. He then instructs students about what to do by way of revision or poses questions that will lead them to make specific changes in the text. He does not shy away from telling students precisely what their writing needs or offering them specific directions for revision" (p. 204).

Here is a brief excerpt from our summary of Gere's style: "Gere's comments never risk taking center stage. If she controls the spotlight, she is intent on throwing the light on the student, not on her role as a responder. Although she determines through her very choice of comments what the student initially may attend to, she leaves it up to the student to decide how to use her suggestions and to find ways to address her concerns. She does not lay out a script to be followed or overtly guide the student about how he might take up the tasks" (p. 236).

We have purposefully made these summaries descriptive rather than evaluative. This is not a matter of right and wrong or good and bad; there is no debate as to whether a teacher will exercise control in responding to student writing; by being a teacher and by means of making marks on a student's

Exhibit 8.1. More Directive Response

Writing 12
Chris B.
Second Rough Draft

Street Gangs: One Point of View

I'm writing this paper on street gangs because I was once part
of one, and I feel that this gives me some authority to write a
legitimate opinion *about them from the inside.*

I never asked or set out to join a gang, | it just happened by
association. I knew some guys who were members of the Cripps and by
hanging around them I was sort of "taken in" by the gang and generally
thought to be a part of them by everyone else.

Unlike some members, I tried to maintain a low profile. I didn't
provoke fights or do destructive things on purpose, but we had a
strong bond. If one person was in trouble, no matter who or what kind
it was, everyone was there regardless, *of the cause. (?)*

This sticking together almost always occurred in a physical sense.
If one of our guys were to be beaten up, the rest of us would take a
revenge of some sort, whether it be by beating someone up or
vandalizing someone's property, we always got even. That was a basic
rule, nobody could "be one up on us", we always had to get even.

Except for this one occasion, I can't really remember us actually
going out and starting trouble for no "reason". We were at the pool,
and what we did was single out one person at a time. Once we had a
target, one of us would go up to that certain someone and "sucker
punch" him and before he could retaliate the rest of the gang would
break it up.

This sentence makes us expect something else. Begin with "On one occasion..."

This is the kind of detail we need. But we need more, even here.

1

Source: Straub and Lunsford, 1995, p. 199.

Exhibit 8.2. Less Directive Response

```
Writing 12
Chris B.
Second Rough Draft
```

                    Street Gangs: One Point of View

    I'm writing this paper on street gangs because I was once part

of one, and I feel that this gives me some authority to write a

legitimate opinion.

Can you start with one specific experience drawn from your life with street gangs?

    I never asked or set out to join a gang, it just happened by

association. I knew some guys who were members of the Cripps and by

hanging around them I was sort of "taken in" by the gang and generally

thought to be a part of them by everyone else.

    Unlike some members I tried to maintain a low profile. I didn't

provoke fights or do destructive things on purpose, but we had a

strong bond. If one person was in trouble, no matter who or what kind

it was, everyone was there regardless.

These ¶'s seem to deal with the issue of "membership." What else can you say about membership in the gang? Is there a way to make connections among these ¶'s?

    This sticking together almost always occured in a physical sense.

If one of our guys were to be beaten up, the rest of us would take a

revenge of some sort, whether it be by beating someone up or

vandalizing someones property, we always got even. That was a basic

rule, nobody could "be one up on us", we always had to get even.

What does this "exception" show? What do you want your readers to draw from this?

    Except for this one occasion, I can't really remember us actually

going out and starting trouble for no "reason". We were at the pool,

and what we did was single out one person at a time. Once we had a

target, one of us would go up to that certain someone and "sucker

punch" him and before he could retaliate the rest of the gang would

break it up.

                                1

Source: Straub and Lunsford, 1995, p. 229.

paper, he or she is controlling. The question, then, is not whether but to what degree the teacher will control. And it should be clear that too little control (that is, guidance) is not necessarily better than too much control. Our teachers strive for balance. But the teaching personas that they present us illustrate a very real range in terms of the control they exercise.

Conclusion: Implications

I will conclude by trying to answer the central question the editors of this collection asked in inviting me to write this chapter: What implications does *12 Readers Reading* have for the ways in which teachers in the disciplines should respond to student writing? I began by enunciating some pretty clear-cut principles for response, notable among them the principle that responses should not take control from the student. But then I complicated matters with the caveat that there is a real range in the control that teachers exercise when it comes to guiding/controlling students. (Were there time, I could complicate every other principle I have offered in a similar fashion.) As I reflect on this complexity, I am reminded of a comment Chris Anson (one of the twelve readers) made in talking about his philosophy of teaching writing:

> Early in my career in composition, . . . I began to listen carefully to the ways students talked about their writing. Those who made the most progress seemed, during the various processes of drafting and revising, very uncertain. They weighed alternatives. They wrestled with rhetorical choices. They shaped, embellished, and rejected directions for their texts. Yet at the same time they seemed to embrace this uncertainty, to relish it.

If we see responding to student writing as a rhetorical act, as it certainly is, it should not be surprising that we find the same kind of complexity and uncertainty that Anson alludes to in this process. We must struggle in every case to communicate as effectively as possible, within the constraints placed on us by that rhetorical situation. One of the most important of those constraints is the teacher's voice. It is obvious that a biology teacher responding to a paper about photosynthesis is not going to sound like an English teacher responding to a paper about a Shakespearean play. Less obvious, but equally important, is the fact that one English or biology teacher is not going to write (and sound) like another English or biology teacher. If there is one thing that *12 Readers Reading* makes clear, this is it.

Having introduced, and embraced, this complexity, I would like to conclude by moving, again, in the direction of simplicity. With apologies to Robert Fulghum,[7] with the understanding of the fact that there is a fine line between simplification and oversimplification, and without saying where exactly I learned them, I would like to enunciate four basic principles for responding to student writing:

Say enough for students to know what you mean. It doesn't do any good, and it can create a great deal of frustration for the student, if he doesn't really know what to make of the comments on his paper.

Don't say too much. Students (and teachers) have a limited amount of time to dedicate to any one paper. There is a point at which overload sets in, and no matter how instructive the comments may be, they do not prove useful to the student.

Don't spend very much time on matters of correctness. It is all right (even good) if teachers in the disciplines communicate to students that correctness matters—by telling them errors hurt the effectiveness of finished products, suggesting they get the necessary help on these matters, and ultimately, counting off if students do not produce edited work. However, teachers in the disciplines should not allow attention to these matters to distract them, or their students, from the role that writing can play in discovering and sharing knowledge in their disciplines.

Focus your attention on understanding what students mean to say. One of your strengths as a teacher in the disciplines is that you are able to understand what the student is saying and let her know when the ideas are good, even if the form and mechanics could be better. Don't lose that strength. A corollary to this principle, of course, is that you should be sure that students "mean" what they say. One of the dangers of knowing the material is that you can interpret what students meant (or what they should have meant) from sentences that don't show, at all, that the student has a grasp of the concept. If students' writing does not make it clear that they know what they are talking about, your comments should invite them to reexamine and rethink what they are saying. However, when it is clear that students have understood important concepts in your discipline, don't lose the opportunity to respond to *what* they are saying.

Notes

1. The twelve teachers in our study are Chris Anson, University of Minnesota; Peter Elbow, University of Massachusetts, Amherst; Anne Ruggles Gere, University of Michigan; Glynda Hull, University of California, Berkeley; Richard L. Larson, Lehman College, City University of New York; Ben McClelland, University of Mississippi; Frank O'Hare, Ohio State University; Jane Peterson, Richland College; Patricia Lambert Stock, Michigan State University; Edward M. White, California State University, San Bernardino; Tilly Warnock, University of Arizona; and the late Donald C. Steward, Kansas State University.

2. Though the student papers were real, the students we presented our readers with were constructs. That is, we created courses for them to be in and personal histories between the teachers of those courses and these individual students. We also allowed our readers to add to this history so as to help us see how their responses were shaped by context.

3. Actually, we complicated this direction a bit further. Realizing that in a situation such as this one, these teachers could not possibly respond to these students as they would were the students in their classes, we settled for asking the teachers to treat the essays as models they might use in training new writing teachers.

4. We label as heuristic those questions that are designed to help the student generate information. A *closed heuristic question* is one that has a clear-cut answer that the teacher knows when he or she asks it. An *open heuristic question* is one that allows the student freedom to find an answer that the teacher does not already know.

5. As the name would suggest, an *interpretive* comment is one in which the teacher allows the student to see how he or she is understanding the text.

6. The *reader experience* comment, much like Peter Elbow's (1981) "movies of the mind," allows the student to know what the teacher is experiencing as a reader of his or her text.

7. I am, of course, referring to Robert Fulghum's *All I Really Need to Know I Learned in Kindergarten* (New York: Villard Books, 1988).

References

Elbow, P. *Writing with Power.* New York: Oxford University Press, 1981.

Straub, R. E., and Lunsford, R. F. *Twelve Readers Reading: Responding to College Student Writing.* Cresskill, N.J.: Hampton Press, 1995.

RONALD F. LUNSFORD is chair and professor of English at the University of North Carolina at Charlotte.

Tape-recorded commentary can help teachers to play a more supportive role in the development of students' writing in different disciplines. Strategies for using the method are presented along with excerpts from students' writing and teachers' taped commentary.

In Our Own Voices: Using Recorded Commentary to Respond to Writing

Chris M. Anson

Voices, Read and Heard

The process of reading and responding to students' work often places us, as teachers, in the role of judges. Typically, we imagine a certain response to our assignments that might count as excellent or accomplished and then read the actual papers against that ideal. Because we have limited time to write on students' papers, we usually focus on the most important shortcomings relative to the ideal, hoping that students will learn by trial and error to avoid the same problems in future assignments.

This role and purpose often yields a formal, authoritative, and judgmental style of response. Early in my own teaching, I felt uneasy using this style in my written comments when my classroom demeanor was more casual and personal. When I commented on students' writing, it was as if I distanced myself from them and turned into a juror, casting legalistic verdicts on their work. Even when I tried to write more openly, in a questioning or supportive way, the very existence of my own text, layered over the students' words and sometimes identifying their errors, seemed controlling and dictatorial.

My discomfort with this type of response was explained, if not eased, by new work in the developing field of composition studies that showed how to make the learning process of writers more central in the classroom. Instead of simply assigning papers and then judging them when they came in, teachers can provide support for writers at various stages during the process, especially between successive drafts. But even with the help of my revision guides and the use of small groups in which students shared drafts of their papers, my response to their work, which I continued to offer in writing at the end of the process, seemed to change little.

NEW DIRECTIONS FOR TEACHING AND LEARNING, no. 69, Spring 1997 © Jossey-Bass Publishers

Then, halfway through a course, one of my students had eye surgery and was told to read as little as possible for a few days. Not wanting to fall behind in her work, she asked if I would be willing to tape-record my comments about a paper she had turned in before the surgery. I agreed and set to work that night.

The experience of talking to my student about her paper on a cassette tape entirely changed the way I now respond to students' written work in most of the classes I teach. The method itself is quite simple; it involves substituting or supplementing the usual written commentary we give to students (in the margins or at the end of their papers) with oral commentary given to them on cassette tapes. When students turn in a draft of final paper, they provide an inexpensive blank cassette tape, appropriately labeled, which the teacher can put into a small carrying case or cassette storage box available at most discount stores. On the day the papers are returned, the students also get back their cassette tape with the teacher's commentary, which they can then listen to when they look over their work.

Tape-recording my comments on students' papers didn't remove the responsibility of making judgments. I was still using my expertise to weigh the students' successes and shortcomings and, on final papers, reach a verdict about their quality. But the tone and style of my comments seemed different. Because I was literally *talking* to each student, I felt a social dimension to my commentary that had been less present in my short, often corrective written remarks. My comments had a narrative quality, and were framed with personal remarks. I found myself starting with brief openers: "Hi, Mark, how's it going? Hey, I love this title!" My written comments, in contrast, lacked context and seemed impersonal—a kind of shorthand. On the tapes, I could loop back to issues earlier in the paper, or explain myself in detail, or allude to class sessions. I could show something of my own reading process, the way I interpreted the student's words or the way I tried to construct meaning from the student's text. Even though I was in most cases grading students' work on the tapes, I also felt a change in my purpose, as what had been correcting and judging eased gently into coaching and advising. I began feeling more like a mentor, a teacher in the true sense of the word. My students seemed to learn more from me, and I learned much more from them—about themselves and what was happening to them over the progress of my courses.

As I experimented with the tape method, I also found that I no longer dreaded the process of reading my students' work. For one thing, I was more comfortable with my role; I felt better about who I was in relation to my students. But I was also astonished to see how much more help I was giving students in my taped comments than in my written marginalia. In just a few minutes, I could offer advice or give readerly response that would have taken me hours to write out by hand. A typical tape of five or ten minutes represented pages of material I would have been incapable of offering as written notes. As I evaluated the method, I also found that students not only preferred taped commentary but rated my overall teaching more highly. The tapes were revealing something about me as a teacher that my students weren't getting from my written comments.

In the fifteen years since I began using this method, I found myself experimenting with various styles and techniques in search of the "best" approach. The experimentation was worthwhile because it showed me the great variety of ways in which we can use our voices to help students. But it also showed me that the best method is at best relative: we must learn to adapt approaches like tape-recorded response to the specific contexts in which we teach. The following are some of the issues I have found most important to consider before I use the method.

Decide whether to comment on drafts or final papers or both. Comments on final papers are usually evaluative. The response explains a grade or other assessment of the writing, sometimes correcting errors or pointing out problems in logic, organization, the adherence to norms of the field, or other concerns. The writing becomes a kind of test—of accumulated knowledge, of the ability to use the methods of intellect or scholarship in a specific field, or of the ability to create clear, readable prose. Taped comments can provide a more thorough, detailed explanation of your assessment, so that students can understand how you arrived at it and can learn from your counsel.

But you can use taped comments even more productively during the students' process of writing a paper, especially when that paper is long and complex. The most effective moment is when a student has finished a full rough draft of a paper. If you build in a requirement for students to submit a rough draft a week or more before the deadline for the final draft, you may find that what they turn in looks surprisingly like what they would have turned in as their final paper. But now, using the tapes, you can provide comments that lead to an improved paper. The learning that results from this intervention is much greater than what students learn from final comments, which they sometimes ignore in their haste to see only the grade.

A student in an introductory psychology course, for example, submitted a draft of a paper on natural selection that included the following paragraph:

Natural selection can effect behavior in the way that people strive to be the best and become selected. Therefore you can change your behavior to get into the selection process. The environment is always changing and we adapt our behavior to the environment. So we are often changing to the environment so we become more a part of the natural selection process.

In his recorded commentary, the teacher said this:

I like the way you're moving from the biological to the, I guess you could call it the social meaning of natural selection in this paragraph, but the leap may be too big here. Maybe you could explain what you mean by being selected, and by getting into the selection process. What would happen if someone was not well suited for the environment, you know, in a biological way, but still got selected? And on getting selected, do you mean by this something social, like being chosen for a team, or something biological, along the lines of animal competition during mate selection? I'm just feeling a little confused at this point.

Decide in advance on your investment of time. Talking out loud about a student's paper seems to spark many spontaneous discoveries that lead to more explanation and more talk. It is easy to spend twenty or thirty minutes on a tape and still feel less than talked out. Depending on how many students you may have or how long and complex are their papers, you may want to limit your talk to a specific amount of time. I usually aim for five minutes, glancing at my watch when I start. As I see the time running out, I wrap up my commentary with a list of the four or five most important issues in the student's paper.

Decide how you will organize your comments. The actual process of talking about a student's text can be quite varied, and each method has different consequences. I have discovered two general approaches: *organizing your commentary* and *reading live.*

Organizing your commentary means knowing what you want to say before you say it. Reading the paper first very quickly to get sense of its contents and structure will help you to formulate your thoughts before turning on the tape recorder. You can even jot down some marginal shorthand during your initial skimming to jog your memory later when you begin to talk (I often use checks, question marks, or circles for this purpose). Then, as you talk, you can focus on the most important issues you noticed during your initial reading. For example, if you discover that a student has not offered any evidence to support a main assertion in a paper, you can address that problem from the start, and suggest ways to revise the draft.

Organizing your thoughts in advance allows you to give students clear, concise commentary usually moving from the most to the least important concerns in the paper. What the commentary gains in these features, however, it often loses in its lack of spontaneity. Tape-recorded commentary also offers you a chance to *show* students what happens in readers' minds as they construct meaning from a piece of writing. In this process, you can read a small part of the paper, usually a paragraph or a section, then comment on what it has done to advance a line of thought or move a paper forward. The pause button found on some tape recorders lets you stop to read the next chunk of text and then continue sharing your experience as a reader. Some users of taped commentary actually read the paper aloud, commenting on it as they read and giving voice to their otherwise internal thoughts and reading experiences. This method clearly takes more time, but is especially effective for writers who lack experience reading their own texts.

The difference between these two approaches is illustrated in excerpts from two teachers' taped commentaries on papers in political science courses. The first excerpt is from the start of one teacher's comments on a paper written by a senior (the paper is about the decentralization of political leadership in Senegal). After some opening remarks and a few comments praising the student's progress, the teacher says this:

OK, what I'd like to do here is to focus on three key, um, three main areas that you should probably consider as you prepare the next draft. First, structure. Second, elaboration, especially in the section on the 1990 reform and the role of PS in the political process. Third, the style of the section describing your research site. OK. On the structure question, I really like your use of these subheadings, but at times I think you've almost got too many. If you take a look on, on page 14 . . .

For this rather long project, and perhaps because the draft had already undergone some development, the teacher decided it would be best to read the entire paper and then organize his comments into three areas for revision. In contrast, another teacher in the same department chose to use the reading live approach. The following excerpt is from about halfway through this teacher's taped response to a paper about the role of the United Nations in promoting international peace. The student had begun each new section with a news headline about the United Nations.

OK. I've moved on now and read the next section on neutrality. One thing I'm noticing right away is the absence of the news item as a leading, ah, as a way to give some background to the section. Do you want to be consistent with this device? Because maybe your reader starts expecting them, you know, I certainly, after five or six of these, I'm really enjoying them and sort of looking for them. You might check my reaction about this against some other readers. See if they feel the same way. OK, I'm also, at this point, I'm thinking, "she's going to link the good offices concept with neutrality. . . ."

In contrast to her colleague, this teacher uses her own experience as a reader to show her student what works or doesn't work for her as she reads. Perhaps because it is not organized in advance, this commentary also seems to put much of the responsibility for decision making back on the student, who must now weight her teacher's reactions against those of other readers and make choices for revision.

Include contextual remarks when appropriate. Written comments on students' papers rarely link the paper to other work, allude to progress in the course, or include remarks about other matters of the classroom context. Due to their narrative quality, taped comments let you mentor students in the full context of your class. Comments can focus on the progress a student has made between the last paper and the one being discussed. It is also easier to focus on the strategies a student has employed to create a paper, especially if you have seen a draft in progress. In a response to a lab report, a teacher said the following:

You've really got the hang of doing the methods sections; this one is a lot clearer than in your last assignment. What I'd work on now is deciding which details to include in your conclusions, because this seems long, and I can't tell as a reader what's important and what's not important in the experiment.

Use the opportunity for explanation. Draining of time and energy, written comments can encourage a brevity that may not always be helpful to students. The marginal label "Awk" (for "awkward") identifies a place where you stumbled over the student's badly crafted language, but the label tells the student nothing about why the passage seems awkward or about how to rethink its wording. When they are strategically placed in a rough draft, such abbreviated comments can help to put the responsibility back on the student for working out a revision. When these comments appear on final drafts, however, students may be puzzled by them or simply ignore them. As a result, students learn little from them.

In taped comments, consider offering some brief descriptions of specific problems. Most helpful are *reader-like* explanations—simply talking through your actual experience reading something that is confusing, illogical, poorly worded, or otherwise problematic. In a response to a rough draft of a history paper, a teacher said this:

> Now, when I got to this line, I stumbled a little. Let me read it to you, OK? "The American Board of Commissioners provided funding for the establishment of permanent missionary schools sponsoring education for Cherokees." I guess I'm wondering if the funding is sponsoring this, or the schools? If it's the schools, as a reader I'm wondering what it means to sponsor education? See the confusion here?

Provide helpful strategies. Perhaps because they take so much time, written comments rarely offer students helpful techniques or strategies for revision, for future writing assignments, or for classwork. In just a few seconds on a tape, you can show students how to overcome difficulties that are apparent in their writing. Reading a lab report in mechanical engineering, a teaching assistant said this:

> Try organizing the observations from most to least important; then draw a line in the list at the point when they stop being essential to your conclusions.

And while reading a psychology paper, another teacher made this comment:

> I guess I want to believe you here but you haven't given me enough reason. I think the issue is causality—what evidence is there that proximity actually causes aggression? So what you might try next time is naming each possible cause on the left side of a piece of paper; then write down the evidence of causality on the right side. Put a question mark next to any items where the research evidence conflicts. Then when you make an assertion, you can say whether it's supported in some way.

Consider students' concerns. Although academic papers are usually supposed to stand on their own, our role as teachers allows us to carry on dialogues with students *about* their papers. Yet we often miss opportunities for such dialogue when we read students' papers. Students may create a paper in isolation, and we may read it similarly cloistered, the quickly written marginal comments standing as our only real connection with the student. Students' concerns, intentions, and goals are invisible to us, sometimes leading to comments that they perceive to be less than relevant or useful.

Tapes give us the chance to hear students' concerns before we read their work. This can be effective at both the draft and final stages of writing. In my smaller classes, I usually ask students to talk to me on their tape for a maximum of three minutes, focusing on their uncertainties or on the specific issues they would like me to address. After quickly reading a student's paper, I then listen to his or her brief comments and record my response to those comments, along with any other important issues not raised by the student. The following excerpt comes from the tape of a linguistics course student whose own concerns gave his teacher plenty to focus on in the return response:

> . . . I'm also wondering if I've said enough about this kid's phonemes. I mean, it sounds to me like I kind of lurch into the next kid without really finishing with the first kid. It just seems incomplete or something. But then by now it's so darned long, I just can't see adding two pages to the analysis.

Encouraging students to focus on what they perceive to be the problems in their drafts also helps them to build the skills of critical reflection and revision. You can answer well-founded concerns, offering your expert perspectives and suggestions.

Consider student dialogues. Revision groups, or *peer conferences,* have become increasingly popular in courses across the curriculum. Students usually read and respond to the drafts of one or two peers, using a list of questions provided by the teacher. On a designated day, the students discuss their reactions in class, offering readings that are especially useful in the revision process.

Lack of class time sometimes makes revision groups impractical. In such cases, consider having students tape-record their responses to each other's drafts, swapping the tapes in class. Hand out a list of guidelines for the taped commentary (how much time to spend, what comments are appropriate, and so on). Such student-to-student dialogues can be excellent ways to build collaborative learning into a course without sacrificing a lot of time during class sessions.

Spoken Response and New Technologies

Before the advent of cassette tape technology, taped responses would have been impractical; most students didn't own reel-to-reel tape recorders, and these were too bulky and awkward in any case. But almost all students now have a cassette tape player at home or in their car, and all colleges and universities can provide them. The small uniform size of the cassettes makes them no less difficult to handle than students' papers themselves.

In the context of computer technology, we are at a moment in history much like the transition to cassette tapes from reel-to-reel tapes. Consequently, we still may be looking somewhat skeptically on the potential of computers to offer useful alternative methods for responding to students' work: they are too bulky or complicated; access is too limited; there are too many different kinds of programs and equipment.

But this time in history is, in fact, just a moment. It is now estimated that over half of U.S. college students have their own personal computers. Within a few years, microcomputer technology will be at the fingertips of virtually every college student, either personally or on campus, and converting disks into different formats and programs will be simple. How or whether we make use of this technology for enhancing our methods of reading students' work is very much up to us, if we can guide and control the process (see Chapter Ten).

Most newer models of personal computers now have the capability to record and/or play back voice recordings, allowing the concept of tape-recorded commentary to be adapted to word processing. In an evolving draft of a long paper on physical therapy, for example, Jennie, one of my students, wrote the following paragraph:

> ⊠ *Balgrist rehabilitation center is located at the University of Zurich in the city of Zurich which is one of the largest cities in Switzerland. Balgrist specializes in rehabilitation for disabilities from paralysis known as paraplegia and tetraplegia in Swiss German or paraplegic and quadriplegic in English.* ⊠ *It is one of the best rehabilitation centers for people with paralysis disorders. Paraplegikers stay for 4–6 months and tetraplegikers stay up to 1 year if needed.*

After opening Jennie's disk on my computer and locating the installment in which this paragraph appeared, I skimmed through her introduction (which was unchanged since my last commentary) and began to read her new text. When I reached this paragraph, I placed my cursor at the beginning of the paragraph and accessed the voice record function in my computer. Clicking on "record," I then spent about forty-five seconds commenting on the information Jennie was providing in this paragraph. Deposited at the start of the paragraph (as shown) was an icon notifying Jennie that a recorded comment was embedded in her text. I then placed the cursor toward the end of the paragraph and offered her some suggestions about the style of her sentences (which tend to stack up modified information awkwardly). A second icon appeared at that point (as shown).

Opening her file on her own, less sophisticated computer at home, Jennie could see my icons in her text. Although she did not have a voice-record function on her computer, she could still click on the icons and hear a playback of my voice. Later, she could simply delete the icons (and the recordings) from the text when she no longer needed them.

In addition to increasingly sophisticated sound capabilities, computers will eventually involve both the recording and playback of video. Microcomputers are available with tiny video cameras that record the user's face for later playback. Using such technology, a student would be able to open up a paper on a disk, click on an icon, and then both hear and see the teacher, whose image appears in a box at the top of the screen. Though this option may seem almost ridiculous to us now, it won't be long before the quality of images improves and their size increases. The technology will offer us something approaching a student-teacher conference.

Conclusion

No method of response—written marginal annotations, taped comments, even a one-way computerized conference in multimedia—will ever surpass the centuries-old method of sitting down with a writer to discuss his or her work. Nor should it. But as our roles and responsibilities become more diverse and more complex, we should be prepared to use available resources in as educationally rich a way as possible in those situations in which they are most useful and practical. For me, taped response has provided one such way to reach out to students through something more than red marks layered over their own words.

CHRIS M. ANSON is professor of English and director of composition at the University of Minnesota.

The authors offer a framework for thinking about the differences
between responding to student writing on-line and off. The newness
of the on-line environment brings existing teaching practice into relief,
permitting reflection and, as needed, change.

Responding to Writing On-Line

Gail E. Hawisher, Charles Moran

Before we begin to consider the particulars of responding to students' writing on-line, we want to lay down what for us have become ground rules, assumptions that we have come to hold after some decades of teaching in on-line and off-line environments.

The first of these ground rules is that good teaching is good teaching: good classroom practice is good classroom practice. Whether teachers are working on-line or off, they need to know how to respond to students' writing. In both real and virtual spaces, teachers need to experience and acquire an inventory of responding strategies so that they can respond flexibly and appropriately to their students' writing—which may come at them in a range of genres and at different stages of composition. So contemporary work on responding to writing—we think here particularly of the categories of response laid out in Peter Elbow and Pat Belanoff's *Sharing and Responding* (1995)—is useful to teachers on-line and off.

The second ground rule arises from the first: on-line responding, if well done, will not save time. Both of us would be appalled at the prefabricated reader-response, on-line or off: the "awk" rubber stamp from the world of paper or the computer file of precast responses that we hear the occasional computer literate teacher speak of as a labor-saving device. And both of us agree that student writers themselves need to be able to say what kind of response they need. On-line or off, this good teaching practice takes time.

Our third ground rule is that students who are required to work on-line must have equal and sufficient access to the on-line workspace. In a conventional classroom, we assume that students have equal access to pen and paper. But because computers and on-line access cost money, computer technology cannot be presumed to be universally and equally distributed. In Charlie Moran's fall 1995 graduate seminar, "Writing and Emerging Technologies," his

NEW DIRECTIONS FOR TEACHING AND LEARNING, no. 69, Spring 1997 © Jossey-Bass Publishers

students—a constituency that one might think would have easy access to his university's on-line spaces—do not have equal access. All have acquired modems and e-mail (electronic mail) accounts, but most have their computers at home and not where they work—in the library and in their offices. Two are teachers in secondary schools. For them, access is always inconvenient, often impossible. Further, Charlie's university provides limited and inconvenient computer access for its citizens. Charlie and his graduate students have therefore decided that they will do their writing and responding off-line.

Gail Hawisher's students, on the other hand, have what many consider easy access. There are 750 computers installed at on-campus sites with additional machines in the dorms and in departmental labs. Her students are able to access e-mail and PacerForum (the conference program she uses) by stopping by the English building's computer site before and after class. She hastens to add that for some students access is not as easy as for others. Not only do several dislike writing in a lab, but two of the undergraduates are returning-women students who travel some distance to campus. At the start of the semester Gail reasoned, perhaps unfairly, that the returning students needed to have as much experience with on-line writing and response as she could offer them. A class without an on-line component would do them no favor. Therefore she and the undergraduate and graduate students in her classes this semester respond to one another on-line, despite the considerable inconvenience for some. Here, Gail has placed her teacherly judgment of need into the equation and used it to argue that access is sufficient, if not equal.

With these ground rules in place, we feel able now to play the game: to say that responding on-line is different from responding off-line. In the pages that follow, we review some of the differences between the two, and we point out some of the features of on-line responding that seem particularly promising. Through this explanation and description runs a theme: that given equal and sufficient access—which is the case at Gail's university and in Charlie's first-year writing course held in a networked classroom—when we begin responding to students' writing on-line, we find that we have been given an opportunity to rethink and reinvent the ways in which we teach. When we begin to work on-line, even minimally, we come to see our present practices in a new light. What was transparent and "natural" off-line becomes suddenly visible and open to reflection on-line. We come to realize that we have made choices, and we find that we now have an opportunity to examine these choices and make change where we deem change to be necessary. As we have ourselves moved on-line, we have found ourselves able to reinvent the ways in which we teach, and the ways in which our students learn, in both our on-line and off-line classrooms.

Apparent Intimacy of On-Line Discourse

Despite the alleged impersonality of the computer screen, on-line communication seems to evoke an intimate and highly personal discourse. Metaphors for on-line communication (both real-time and e-mail) are almost always social: the "parlor" or the house with many parlors (Howard, 1992), "chat rooms," or "forums" (Malone, 1994). When we read the written language—a book, a letter—we make contact with a person, the author, certainly, but we meet that author as we would meet a public lecturer in public dress: presentable, considered, careful; whereas on-line, we tend to meet authors who have dashed off first thoughts perhaps later to be reconsidered: the mind in dishabille, not yet ready to appear in public.

Thus a teacher's *e-response* will likely be, or become over time, more intimate, more informal, than on-paper response. But teachers have always had the option of being informal. On-line, it is likely that students' responses to the teacher, and to one another, will be informal as well—something that teachers may not welcome or be prepared for. We're thinking here of an e-mail message one of the authors received while working on this chapter. A student (we'll call him "Jim") e-mailed a proposal for a paper and asked for a response. He wrote at the end of the message:

> *Okay, that's a much more detailed proposal than I intended. Have a good weekend, and I guess either e-mail me (I can and do check my account from my dorm) at [e-mail address], or call me (my ph# is 244–8765, and I'm generally up by 8:30 on the weekends, and until midnight). Thank you, Jim (another goofy midwesterner).*

Now certainly this response is properly polite, and it comes at the end of a rather formal proposal for an argumentative paper. But some of the customary rules governing student and teacher interaction have been rewritten: the student is telling the teacher what to do ("call me"), which is fine but not usual, and the teacher now knows the student's weekend sleeping habits, not something she's usually privy to. It's also interesting that the student gives the teacher the option of using the telephone instead of e-mail, not willing to trust the new medium entirely. In his first semester, he's still somewhat anxious about the network's reliability.

This potential intimacy is a two-edged sword. For teachers with established authority—tenured professors, for example—the chance to chat with students, and have the students chat back, may be a welcome deflection of the teacher's institutional authority. For a brand-new young teacher, and even more so for a teaching assistant or a part-time lecturer with little institutional authority, this opportunity for informal discourse may not be welcome at all. A young and/or marginalized teacher may require more distance than electronic discourse may seem to provide. In a study of teachers' on-line and off-line personae, Carbone and others (1993) found that often teachers' on-line voices complemented their off-line voices. A teacher who was warm and open in off-line relations with students was reserved and businesslike on-line; another teacher who was reserved off-line was warm and playful on-line.

Conventions governing on-line discourse will have to be created consciously by the teacher and by the classroom community. Conventions governing classroom behavior are of course always under negotiation, off-line or on. But in the conventional classroom, the teacher can draw on the students' previous experience—perhaps we should call it training?—in K–12 schooling. In the conventional classroom, this training has been associated with an array of visual cues that the teacher can use to signal expected behavior. The teacher can, for example, place the chairs in a circle, indicating a wish to reduce the hierarchical distance between teacher and student. Or the teacher can create a teacher-place, a desk or table that is both distant and different from the students' workspace, indicating a wish to establish and confirm the institutionally conferred distance between teacher and student. Off-line, we have visual cues, stage props, symbols of institutional power: the teacher's desk, the clock, the lectern, the gradebook, perhaps even the American flag! On-line, we usually have, for now, written language alone. In the new medium, the teacher and student together will have to establish what is, and what is not, appropriate behavior.

Public Nature of On-Line Discourse

Paradoxically, on-line communication is public as well as intimate. One of the principal differences between electronic text and print is that electronic text can be copied without measurable cost and effort. Potentially, therefore, all class writings are publishable, made instantly available to all. Because this potential is there, it will be exercised. Charlie makes his on-line responses to his students' writing semipublic, a behavior that his students have come to accept as normal. He leaves his responses to their writing in read-only files that are accessible not only to the student he is responding to but to other students in the class. Charlie feels that by going public in this way he is modeling a wide range of responding techniques. In addition, his dialogues with individual students become part of the discourse of the class as a whole, not private transactions between teacher and student. Charlie feels that this is a positive change for him, and he now prefers to make his responses public documents even in off-line teaching situations. In his current off-line graduate seminar, he photocopies and distributes not only his students' writing but his comments on that writing, a practice that has grown from his experience teaching in a computer-equipped classroom. He notes that now he would rather not say anything to a particular student that should not be read by others. Here, the on-line classroom has begun to shape off-line teaching practice.

In addition to teaching in computer classrooms, Gail, too, teaches classes in conventional classrooms but with a substantial on-line component. She sets up a student *e-forum* for each student writing group, accessible only to those in that group. The e-forum becomes something of a group conference meeting between the teacher and a few classmates. Because of the success of the e-forums, Gail has begun holding face-to-face group conferences with students, thus borrowing an on-line practice for off-line teaching. At these forums—whether on- or off-line—students decide what shape their group project will take, what kinds of on-line participation the class will engage in, how they will respond to one another's writing, and how group members will present their project to the whole class. They also post parts of their project, expecting group members to comment on their efforts. The group e-forums, like off-line writing groups, are in addition to the larger on-line and off-line class discussions.

The text generated in the ways described here is public—and remarkably durable. It can last for years on a system, depending upon the teacher's need to clean the virtual desk. Further, teachers need to remember that all systems have a sysop (system operator), and more likely a number of people who have special access to all files in the host computer. This sysop can, at least theoretically, read every piece of text that is on the system. We have to remember, therefore, that this e-mail that seems so intimate and personal is really much more public than teachers and students may think as they write and read on-line. As we have noted elsewhere, e-mail does not have an envelope (Hawisher and Moran, 1993).

Rhythms of Response

E-mail or on-line communication is fast—if everything is working right and if both students and teacher have regular access to terminals. At least for the beginning user, e-mail creates the impression of instant transmission: when the writer hits the Enter key and sends the text, the writer imagines that through the magic of electronic communication the writer-reader transaction is complete. It has been documented that on-line writers expect a rapid response (Feenberg, 1989). And it may be that the teacher can respond quickly some of the time. We know of one teacher who instructs her students to put drafts in a special electronic homework folder. Because her students tend to work late at night and she tends to work early in the morning, they leave material that she responds to sometimes not long after they go to bed. When the students get up in the morning, the teacher's comments are there waiting for them (Rebecca Howard, e-mail message to Gail Hawisher, Feb. 14, 1994.)

Our experience has been that teachers responding on-line will either have to respond quickly to their student writers or will have to try to establish conventions that work against this apparent property of the medium. E-response carries with it the possibility of text overload, for teacher and for student. If we do not find ways to structure the campuswide use of on-line response, we fear that instructors may find themselves faced with new demands added to already heavy workloads. Five years from now, we may regard on-line response as invisible work, work that's expected but performed without notice or pay, work that is, in effect *telework*.

Telework, a term more likely to be heard in business organizations than in the academy, has always been part of the writing instructor's life. Sproull and Kiesler (1988) describe telework as an at-home continuation or extension of office work. Traditionally, writing teachers do homework: preparing for classes, reading and responding to student papers, recording grades. They don't, traditionally, spend much time talking to students on the telephone, visiting with them, or communicating with them in other ways. On-line communication increases the teacher's accessibility and can therefore bring additional work to the teacher's "desk."

What is true for the teacher is true for the student as well: using distribution lists, a teacher can, with a keystroke or two, send multiple copies of an electronic response to an entire class. Students in on-line peer groups can also easily and rapidly create a huge volume of text for one another. As instructors, we will need to find ways of establishing limits, for ourselves and for our students, if the on-line world is to remain manageable and useful for our teaching and their learning.

Flaming

Since the inception of the on-line medium, observers have noted that on-line writers tend to respond not only quickly but without as much restraint as they would if they were corresponding on paper (Shapiro and Anderson, 1985; Sproull and Kiesler, 1988). In extreme cases the lack of restraint becomes "flaming," using inappropriate and hurtful on-line language. We know of one instructor who first tried to use e-response to teach his entire class. Before long, his class rebelled, and students were sending messages that asked, "How's your sex life, Teach?" This behavior was unacceptable to the instructor and certainly would not be acceptable to us. Since the early mutiny (Kremers, 1988), the instructor has changed his tactics and now makes great use of one-on-one teaching using e-response (Kremers, 1993). He reports that now, having established these limits, both he and his students are able to engage in "substantive, extended conversations" that look nothing like the wild free-for-all he first encountered. Such lack of restraint has been attributed to the medium's lack of social cues (Sproull and Kiesler, 1988), an argument that has been disputed by other researchers (Spears and Lea, 1992).

For us, the possibility of *inadvertent* flaming is at least partly a function of the speed with which e-mail responses can be composed and sent. It is also a function of the paradoxically permanent nature of electronic messages. Once an e-mail message has been sent, it cannot be ripped up and redone; it cannot be retracted. It shares this characteristic with speech. Clearly, this aspect of on-line communication presents a danger for a teacher, who will not want to flame students, however inadvertently. A teacher may want to queue messages before sending and review them for any unintentional hurtful comments.

The conventions that we ourselves have established for off-line classroom discourse have been practiced and internalized by our students—and by us—during thirteen years' experience in off-line K–12 classrooms. In setting up on-line writing and responding procedures, to the extent that this is new territory to the participants, it will be necessary for teachers to bring the conventions that they have for off-line classroom discourse into the open, for discussion.

To the extent that teacher and students have learned on-line behaviors in list-servs and discussion groups, they will have to decide consciously which of these behaviors is appropriate to, and which need to be modified for, their on-line work with one another.

Spoken and Written Language

Although it is written, on-line communication tends to be more like the spoken than the written language. Indeed, much of the literature on on-line communication uses the metaphor of speech, not the written language: chat programs, conferences, parlors, virtual spaces for talk and conversation. But e-spaces also have the advantage of being totally textualized environments. Although the discourse may seem like talk, with its rapid exchange of short bits of language, on-line, for now, everyone is writing. But this is not writing to be collected and read later by the teacher. It is writing that has an immediate audience. Students who have come to distrust writing to the teacher and students who refrain from speaking up in class can sometimes find a place in this new context for discourse. In an on-line environment, language is informal, fluid, playful, evanescent, social, give-and-take—interactive in a way that a book does not usually want to be.

This chatty nature of on-line discourse is disturbing to some instructors, and some students, who deplore the volumes of what seems to them to be on-line junk. Again, teachers and students together will have to agree on conventions. For example, will it be OK for a student to leave typos in an on-line peer response? Will it be OK for a teacher to do so? Is "OK" an acceptable on-line convention? Will it be the case that some on-line writing can be chatty and informal and other on-line writing not? If the production and reception of imperfect writing is seen to be a negative learning experience for writers, then it follows that on-line prose will be held to the same standards that final paper drafts are held to. If, however, the on-line environment is seen to be a place where writers can take risks and grow through the risk-taking experience, then on-line prose will be held to a different standard than final paper drafts.

To paraphrase one of our student writers, Will on-line responding "count"? Will the informal writing have a deadline? Will it have to be turned in at a particular time? Or will it count in the way that class participation is often counted, in some vague way an indicator of one's engagement in the work of the semester? Whether the instructor regards the on-line writing as print or talk can make a huge difference in students' perceptions of the value of their on-line activity (Eldred and Fortune, 1992).

Both of us have also experimented with the on-line assignment, which, predictably perhaps, changes the criteria by which instructors judge paper assignments. We describe one assignment here, a recent analytical piece that students were to write while Gail was out of town. She promised to read and respond to their analyses on the road. The assignment was this:

Take either a recent copy of WIRED magazine in print or its WWW counterpart, HotWired. Look it over, read some of the articles, scrutinize the images, and decide for whom the magazine or Web site seems intended and whether it has value for you and/or for your teaching. I'd then like you to decide how—if at all—you might use the 'zine in your classes. Post an extended argument either for or against its pedagogical utility.

The students wrote rather lengthy on-line responses (perhaps 250 words or so), short for paper but long for e-spaces. Gail read each, one after the other, rather perfunctorily until she reached the fourth response. It was addressed to a student we will call "Chris" and was a response to the preceding response.

Chris, although I have no idea what you mean by "quasi-ridiculous" and "inefficiently speculative," I would disagree that the articles are useless for classes. . . . In fact, I thought I'd discuss the gender issue thing—it just so happens that my issue contains a letter critiquing WIRED for its white-maleness.

This response was the first to indicate that students were reading one another's entries. Until then, the responses were just there, with nothing to suggest that students were discussing the issues as Gail had hoped they would. Until they started talking back to one another, Gail considered the assignment a flop. Talking back may not be a customary criterion for off-line writing, but it surely is for many electronic classes. On-line, the teacher's criteria for the success of an assignment change, and with the changed criteria come new possible teacher-student relationships.

Collaboration, Group Work, and On-Line Response

As we noted earlier, on-line the distinction between student and teacher has to be constructed anew, in the absence of the cues that furnish the off-line classroom. Left to itself, the chatty, social nature of on-line communication lends itself to collaboration, cooperation, group work, and group response (Harasim, 1989). Further, the quick turnaround of electronic communication makes cooperation and collaboration much easier. We note, for example, that this collaboratively written chapter went through five drafts on one Sunday afternoon, the text moving back and forth between Urbana, Illinois, and Amherst, Massachusetts, at something like the speed of light, first one of us adding and editing and then the other. The culture of on-line communication does not accept as easily as does the culture of print the idea of the single author.

Perhaps for this reason, shortly after he began teaching in computer-equipped networked classrooms, Charlie Moran found himself defining group tasks and work schedules for his students, moving them toward collaborative projects. In off-line classrooms he had published his students' writing every two weeks, collecting their final drafts, providing a cover and table of contents,

numbering the pages, and taking the whole stack of manuscripts off to be pho-
tocopied. Once in the on-line classrooms, he and his fellow on-line teachers
continued to publish printed anthologies of student writing, but they distributed the work differently. They divided students into editing teams, each group
of four students responsible for issuing a call for manuscripts, establishing
deadlines, determining the extent to which they were going to edit the manuscripts that did come in, and distributing tasks such as the creation of a cover,
table of contents, and introduction. Since that time, Charlie and his first-
year students have collaboratively written a book chapter, edited materials
from his university's admissions office, and written a letter to the director of
another writing program evaluating the students' experience of the on-line
writing classroom. Other teachers and students in the same program have
completed collaborative writing and editing tasks for community organizations
and businesses.

Our accumulated experience as teachers, and some research as well (for
example, Harasim, 1989), argues that teaching and learning on-line are most
likely to be social: groups working on tasks defined by the teacher and/or students and modified by the groups; teacher and students together moving
toward some jointly authored and jointly produced task. To the extent that
this is so, the teacher of an on-line class or a class with an on-line component
is likely to conceive of the "course" as a number of tasks to be accomplished,
perhaps by single authors with a great deal of on-line help and feedback from
their peers or perhaps by workgroups who will need to define and assign
tasks.

In this collaborative task-oriented workplace, response to writing begins
to disappear as a discrete category. When the student editors of a class "magazine" dialogue with their authors, they are, of course, responding to writing,
but they are doing so in the context of a task. Their peer response sessions, on-
line and off, are self-generated and scheduled. Their response to one another
is sometimes by written paper note or marginal annotation, sometimes viva
voce, sometimes by on-line message. Most often, this responding is not visible
to the teacher or preserved in some way that would make detailed record keeping possible. The medium has changed the phenomenon. There is software
that mimics paper, providing margins, columns outside the text-column, for
teacher and peer responses. But these columns quickly become the sites for informal dialogue between student and teacher; and columns designated for peer
group work soon turn into a conversation among classmates.

Here, the teacher's response to student work becomes part of an organic
process. Each responder becomes one among many—certainly the teacher is
still the teacher, but to the extent that students own their publication, the
teacher becomes just another reader. The medium further diminishes the
authority of the teacher's response: all responses appear in the same format and
on the same screen. Off-line, there is a clear difference between peer response
and teacher response: one is handwritten and the other sometimes typed; one
is advisory and the other evaluative. On-line, the peer response and teacher

124   WRITING TO LEARN

response will look very much alike. This is yet another situation that student and teacher will have to grapple with in on-line responding.

Conclusion

Our experience suggests to us that although on-line responding is not without its dangers and difficulties, it is certainly territory worth exploring, if only because it is new territory. On-line response does not carry, for now, the baggage that students and teachers may bring to on-paper response: years of writing and receiving marginal comments, years of giving and receiving papers with errors marked. As teachers, so long as we work on paper we may be drawn to the grading and correcting practices we experienced ourselves as students. As students, so long as we receive corrected papers, we may just tag along and play the old game. On-line, both we and our students get a second chance, a chance to reinvent the teacher-writer relationship.

References

Carbone, N., Daisley, M., Federenko, E., McComas, D., Moran, C., Ostermiller, D., and Vanden Akker, S. "Writing Ourselves On-Line." *Computers and Composition,* 1993, *10,* 29–48.
Elbow, P., and Belanoff, P. *Sharing and Responding.* New York: McGraw-Hill, 1995.
Eldred, J., and Fortune, R. "Exploring the Implications of Metaphors for Computer Networks and Hypermedia." In G. E. Hawisher and P. LeBlanc (eds.), *Re-Imagining Computers and Composition: Teaching and Research in the Virtual Age.* Portsmouth, N.H.: Boynton/Cook, 1992.
Feenberg, A. "The Written World." In R. Mason and A. Kaye (eds.), *Mindweave.* New York: Pergamon Press, 1989.
Harasim, L. "On-Line Education: A New Domain." In R. Mason and A. Kaye (eds.), *Mindweave.* New York: Pergamon Press, 1989.
Hawisher, G. E., and Moran, C. "Electronic Mail and the Writing Instructor." *College English,* 1993, *55,* 627–643.
Howard, T. "A Rhetoric of Electronic Communities." Unpublished doctoral dissertation, Purdue University, 1992.
Kremers, M. "Adams Sherman Hill Meets ENFI: An Inquiry and a Retrospective." *Computers and Composition,* 1988, *5,* 69–77.
Kremers, M. "Student Authority and Teacher Freedom." In B. Bruce, J. Peyton, and T. Batson (eds.), *Network-Based Classrooms.* New York: Cambridge University Press, 1993.
Malone, M. S. "Conference Rooms at the Cyberspace Inn." *Sunday New York Times,* May 29, 1994, p. F-21.
Shapiro, N. Z., and Anderson, R. H. *Towards an Ethics and Etiquette for Electronic Mail.* Santa Monica, Calif.: Rand Corporation, 1985.
Spears, R., and Lea, M. "Social Influence and the Influence of the 'Social' in Computer-Mediated Communication." In M. Lea (ed.), *Contexts of Computer-Mediated Communication.* New York: Harvester/Wheatsheaf, 1992.
Sproull, L., and Kiesler, S. "Reducing Social Context Cues: Electronic Mail in Organizational Communication." In I. Greif (ed.), *Computer-Supported Cooperative Work: A Book of Readings.* San Mateo, Calif.: Morgan Kaufmann, 1988.

GAIL E. HAWISHER is professor of English and director of the Center for Writing Studies at the University of Illinois, Urbana-Champaign.

CHARLES MORAN is professor of English and codirector of the Western Massachusetts Writing Project at the University of Massachusetts, Amherst.

This chapter suggests two ways to make the grading of writing easier, fairer, and more helpful for students: using minimal grades or fewer levels of quality, and using criteria that spell out the features of good writing that we are looking for in the assignment.

Grading Student Writing: Making It Simpler, Fairer, Clearer

Peter Elbow

I see three main problems involved in trying to grade writing. First is the plain *difficulty* for us in trying to figure out the grades. For each essay in the stack, we have to decide between A, A-, B+, B, B-, C+, and so forth. If we use the full set of grades, we are using eleven levels (thirteen if we use A+ and D-). Even if we never use *any* grades below C-, we are still having to make fine evaluative discriminations among eight levels. I am relieved to discover how many other faculty members admit to their struggles and frustration with trying to grade writing.

Second (and this helps explain why grading is hard), we know that these decisions are not trustworthy, no matter how hard we agonize. Careful research has demonstrated over and over what common sense has told us—and what our students have learned through controlled experiments of submitting the same paper to different teachers: good teachers and evaluators routinely disagree about grades—and disagree widely. Even a somewhat conservative defender of grades like Edward White (1990) warns of the danger of believing there is such a thing as a "true grade" or "right grade" for a piece of writing.

Third, grading tends to undermine the climate for teaching and learning. Once we start grading their work, students are tempted to study or work for the grade rather than for learning. They see writing as an exercise in trying to say "what teachers want" rather than working out their own thinking. Students resent the grades we give or haggle over them and, in general, see us as people they have to deceive and hide from rather than people they want to take into their confidence.

I don't see any way we can fully *eliminate* these problems if we grade at all (and I am not proposing to give up grading altogether—in this chapter). But I

NEW DIRECTIONS FOR TEACHING AND LEARNING, no. 69, Spring 1997 © Jossey-Bass Publishers

think I can suggest two major ways to *lessen* these problems: minimal grading and giving grades more meaning.

Minimal Grading

Using Minimal Grades on Low Stakes Writing. Minimal grading has always been around, but it is much more common now because so many teachers in so many disciplines use low stakes writing: frequent informal assignments designed to get students to reflect on what they are learning from discussions, readings, lectures, and their own thinking—assignments that count for credit but that individually, don't bear *heavily* on the final course grade.

Thus minimal grading is often the result of crude pragmatic pressures. These faculty who use writing for learning are often not writing teachers, and they are often teaching large classes that are not writing courses. As a result, these faculty often feel they cannot grade student writing carefully or elaborately—and they don't feel obliged to do so because the pieces of writing don't count so much. In this situation, these faculty members have turned to a variety of forms of minimal grading:

A scale with three levels: for example, strong/satisfactory/weak or excellent/OK/no credit.

A scale with two levels: for example, pass/fail, satisfactory/no credit, or check/minus.

A "scale" with only one level: the assignment is acceptable if it is simply turned in at all.

A zero scale: faculty members sometimes don't even collect some pieces of writing-to-learn. On these occasions, they simply ask students to freewrite at the beginning of class about the homework reading—perhaps in relation to a topic for the day—or to write at the end of the class about the day's discussion or lecture, or to write in the middle of a class about an issue that has come up, especially when a discussion goes dead.

Faculty members often don't make any comments at all on this writing. Thus the most obvious advantage of minimal grading is simplicity. It's much less onerous to read lots of student writing when the grade is quick and easy to give and we don't have to comment.

But there are also advantages for student learning. Even though minimal grading removes the incentive to strive for an A for excellence (though we get a fair amount of this incentive if we use a three-level scale), we get to ask students to write far *more* than if we had to grade everything carefully. We get to ask them to think actively about far more of the course material. They have to answer the questions, get their thoughts into writing—yet they don't have to worry so much about whether they are writing in the way that the teacher likes or saying what the teacher agrees with.

Some people complain that minimal grading takes away motivation, but when students struggle for excellence *only* for the sake of a grade, what we see is not motivation but the atrophy of motivation: the gradual decline of the ability to work or think or wonder under one's own steam. Minimal grading on low stakes assignments, however, is a way to help students gradually develop a bit of *intrinsic* motivation—develop a bit of their own curiosity and standards. They get a time out from their habitual and understandable preoccupation with "What is the teacher looking for?" They get a chance to ask themselves, "What am *I* looking for? What do I think? What are my standards?" Of course, students nurtured in a grading economy often need *some* extrinsic motivation to get them working. But that's exactly what minimal grading provides. It makes them *do* the writing and engage the material, but it gives them a lot of choice about *how.* Thus they get small protected spaces for gradually developing small bits of intrinsic motivation. And of course, they still have some high stakes assignments that we grade in a high stakes way—assignments where *we* provide most of the motivation. (I have written more in Chapter One about the advantages of low stakes writing.)

A few students are confused at first by this dialectic between low stakes and high stakes grading. Despite my explanations and warnings, they are caught off balance the first time I use high stakes grading on a high stakes essay. They assume that because I started off with low stakes grading for a number of assignments, I am a "low stakes kind of a guy"—for students often pigeonhole teachers as *either* high *or* low stakes in their approach, as either "hard" or "soft." I find I have to be extremely explicit and even repetitive to help them realize that this whole approach enacts a dialectic. Indeed, I like to bring in the word *dialectic* and talk about the psychological and intellectual benefits of unresolved contraries. But I have learned also to be more blunt and say, "Perhaps you better think of my grading policy as *schizophrenic.*"

Before concluding this section, let me make a point of strategy about *introducing* minimal grading on low stakes writing at the beginning of a course. I always start with a two-level scheme such as pass/fail or satisfactory/No credit. I don't start with the three-level scale because I don't want students to become preoccupied with getting that grade of strong or excellent—preoccupied with trying to figure out what I am looking for; I don't want them to fall back into writing for the grade instead of writing for exploration or learning. And I don't start with no grading at all (accepting anything they turn in or not even collecting the writing at all) because I need to exert *some* pressure in the beginning to engage or focus their efforts. Otherwise, students who have never done this kind of writing are too tempted not to try at all. In short, I start with two-level grading because I want to teach an important skill that interestingly is somewhat rare in students: how to write about an academic topic with their mind focused *wholly* on the topic and issues—and not on how the writing will be graded. Without that skill, it is hard for them to experience satisfaction or even pleasure in writing seriously about something they are studying.

After students have done three to five pieces of low stakes writing graded on a two-level scale—that is, with a great deal of leeway but still a threat of no credit for goofing off—I can move my minimal grading in either direction if it suits me. I can do some low stakes writing in class that I don't even collect—and trust that they will make good academic use of the time. And I can sometimes use a three-level scale to push some of them harder with the reward of excellence—and trust that they won't just clench or become too preoccupied with what the teacher wants and style. But in fact, I often stick with the simplicity of two-level grading throughout the semester.

Using Minimal Grades on High Stakes Writing. We tend to link minimal grading with low stakes writing. That is, we tend to assume that if we want to raise the stakes of the writing and make students strive harder, we should grade on more levels. Conventional A through F grades *feel* more serious.

But this assumption is mistaken. After all, some teachers *do* grade low stakes assignments with the eleven levels of conventional grades. More importantly, we *can* grade high stakes writing assignments with minimal levels. For example, at M.I.T. for the last twenty years or so, faculty have given nothing but pass and fail as final grades to all first-year students in all courses. The stakes are very high indeed and so are the standards, but only two levels are used.

The important strategic point here is that stakes and levels are two quite different dimensions of grading. We will have a much better time grading high stakes assignments if we decouple them—sever the unconscious link between them—and realize that grading always involves two very different questions: How much credit is at stake in this performance? How many levels or grades shall I use on my evaluation scale?

It is true that if we add more levels we add more opportunities to record excellence or distinction. But this also means more competition, more hierarchy, more pecking order—fewer people in same boat. My point here is that increasing the number of levels and giving students the chance to get an A rather than a pass doesn't always succeed in making students work harder:

- The stakes have to be high enough to make extra effort worth expending. Why work hard for an A if it has very little effect on your final grade? A few students work hard for a low stakes A, but usually it's only because they are interested or eager to learn—not merely because of the chance to get an A rather than a pass.
- A fair number of students don't feel an A is within their reach. Sometimes these students will work harder for a strong or even for a demanding pass than for the B-'s and C+'s they are accustomed to getting—grades that they experience as a put-down.
- Some students are simply turned off or thrown off stride by the competition itself.
- Finally, there are students who know they *can* get A's, but they don't care enough to work for them. Many students settle for doing mediocre work

because of their feelings about the course or the conditions in their lives. It's amazing what good work most students can do when they really work hard under supportive conditions. (There are many cases of students wrongly accused of plagiarism because their teachers didn't think they were capable of such good work.)

In short, if our goal is to get students to work harder and more carefully on certain pieces of writing, increasing the number of levels in our grading scale is a very uncertain engine for getting there. But it is a *certain* engine for making *us* work harder. More levels mean more discriminations to make—discriminations that by the same token are harder to make because they are more fine grained and therefore more debatable. In making these finer distinctions, we are providing students with more occasions to dispute and resent the very grades we struggled so hard to determine ("What do you mean B minus? That was a solid B!").

We have a far better chance of getting students to work hard and carefully if we raise the stakes—and then think more strategically about raising the number of levels only a little bit or even not at all. This means not increasing our workload so much and not giving students so many opportunities to resent or quarrel with our grades. If we pursue this approach, we have two important variables we can manipulate.

1. We can make a strategic choice about how many levels to use—even within minimal grading. Two levels is easiest for us, but it doesn't give much scope or incentive. If we move to three levels (for example, strong/satisfactory/weak), we give much more incentive—yet increase our work only a little. Some teachers use four levels (for example, poor/fair/good/excellent). This gives them a lot more work than three levels and provides students more occasions for disagreement or resentment—and yet even four levels is easier than conventional grading.

2. We can make a strategic choice about where to put the borderline between levels—about, that is, how high we set the bar. When I wrote in the previous paragraph that a two-level scale didn't "give much scope or incentive," I was sliding along with a conventional easygoing assumption that "pass/fail means no sweat." This assumption comes from low stakes writing. But there is no law that passing has to be easy—especially for high stakes writing. A higher threshold or demand can be natural and appropriate. Note that even a two-level scale can be very demanding if we raise the bar (as at M.I.T.). If we use three levels, we have even more scope for making strategic decisions about where to place the bars.

Notice, by the way, that with low stakes assignments we can get away with quietly slipping the bar up and down a bit depending on the student. That is, we can tacitly insist that skilled and well-prepared students do a better job for satisfactory than unskilled students with a weak background who are trying hard and improving. When the stakes are low, students aren't likely to mind or even notice a little bit of this kind of flexibility—as long as we make it possible for all students to get a satisfactory without inordinate effort. I at least don't want to push students so hard on low stakes assignments that I lose the essential benefit: that they must engage the material seriously but still get to risk and explore—and that *we* don't have to work too hard in applying the standards.

In this section, then, I'm suggesting that even though we associate minimal grading with low stakes assignments, it is also appropriate and helpful for high stakes assignments. We have the option of raising the stakes and yet keeping down the number of levels in our grading. Such pragmatic considerations are particularly important for large classes. If we are looking at a big stack of papers, think about the difference between giving each one a conventional grade and just picking out the ones that are notably strong or notably weak (that is, using a three-level scale).

Minimal Grading and the Final Grade. At this point, some readers will naturally ask, "But how can I calculate a conventional grade for the course if I only have minimal grades to work with?" This problem brings up another important variable in grading: the number of assignments we grade. If we only have two or three graded assignments and they are graded on only two or three levels, then we have no basis for calculating the final grade for the course. But if we have *lots* of minimal grades—which is easy and natural with lots of low stakes assignments—then it is no problem to derive a conventional final grade.

Take an extreme example. Suppose we have a course with weekly low stakes writing assignments judged on a two-level scale, two high stakes essays judged on a three-level scale, and a conventional final exam judged on a three- or four-level scale. (It's not so hard or unreliable to use four levels for an exam if the exam contains multiple answers.) We can easily calculate a final course grade as follows: students who have a satisfactory on all the low stakes pieces start off with a foundation of B. Then the two high stakes essays and the exam determine whether their B gets pulled up or down. Students who don't have consistently satisfactory work on their weekly low stakes pieces start off from a lower foundation, and they are similarly pulled up or down by their high stakes work.

In this formula, I give quite a lot of emphasis to the low stakes assignments: individually, their weight is low, but in sum, they count for a lot. I want my students to take these pieces seriously—that is, to work hard—but not in a worrying way. Not everyone will agree with my priorities here, but there are obviously other simple formulas one could use for this situation. I just want to illustrate that we can easily derive a maximum-level final grade from minimum-level constituent grades. And I didn't even talk about other factors that many of us feel are important ingredients in calculating a final grade: attendance, participation, effort, and improvement.

Portfolios. Portfolios can be a big help in deriving a conventional final grade from a pool of minimal grades. To decide whether an individual piece of writing is a B or a B- is, in my view, to produce a worthless decision. To decide whether a *portfolio* of writing is a B or a B- is more justifiable: with fuller and richer data, we are justified in trying for a fuller richer discrimination. (And yet I still wouldn't try for such fine discriminations in grading a portfolio—and in fact it turns out that professional readers of portfolios tend to disagree with each other in their grading as much as readers of individual papers. I think it makes more sense to use minimal grading on portfolios too, and then let this minimal yet high stakes portfolio grade be one among various factors in calculating a final conventional grade.)

The real value of portfolio grading is not for precision but for enhancing learning. Portfolios give us a way to get students to look back over all their work for the course and reflect carefully on what they have learned—and even to analyze their learning process. For the most important piece in a portfolio is the reflective essay on the contents of the portfolio.

Portfolios are probably not so feasible for very large classes. You can't even *carry* one hundred portfolios back to your office. But in a large class, it makes perfect sense to ask students to *keep a portfolio* and then at the end to look back at it analytically and write a reflective or analytic essay about their learning and writing. (Some teachers even ask students to suggest a final grade in this final essay of self-analysis.) For low stakes assignments create much more learning if we ask students to gather them all together at the end and work out the most important insights they can—both about the course material and about their processes of learning, thinking, and writing. (See Fulwiler's suggestion in Chapter Two for a portfolio of letters written throughout the course.) Low stakes writing provides students a particularly good window for reflecting on their own habits of thinking and using language. And I love the way portfolios permit me to invite students to put some of their low stakes writing into the final high stakes portfolio—a satisfying thing to do because some of their low stakes writing is often very good. (Readers who want to open the door into the rich literature on portfolios can start with the Belanoff and Dickson, 1991, and Yancey, 1992, collections.)

Contracts for Grading. A contract makes the final grade easy—indeed almost automatic—even if one uses minimal grades during the semester. A contract says, in effect, "If you do X, Y, and Z, you can count on such and such a grade." The point of a contract is to focus less on trying to measure degrees of quality of writing and instead to emphasize *activities* and *behaviors* that will lead to learning.[1]

Teachers tend to think of grading as a way to produce behavior or even motivation for behavior, but notice how it is an *indirect* way of doing so. That is, we hope that the awarding of fair grades will cause students to engage in the learning activities we want them to engage in. Why not instead be more direct with a contract and just, as it were, *make* them do the things that we think will lead to learning? I would rather put my effort into trying to figure out which activities will lead to learning than into trying to measure the exact quality of the final product students turn in.

Objections to Minimal Grading. *"We already use minimal grading: most faculty already give nothing but A's and B's."* I would reply that it is exactly this restricted use of the grading scale that has exacerbated two intertwined problems: grade inflation and grade meaninglessness. When some faculty members give a full range of grades and others give mostly A's and B's, we have a situation of semantic chaos. The grade of B has become particularly ambiguous. For some faculty members, it means "good strong competent work"—and they point out that B is an official honors grade in most college and university catalogues. But when other faculty members give a B they mean "disappointing, second-rate work." And students tend to interpret B as unsatisfactory. If instead of A and B, teachers would use honest words like excellent, honors, outstanding, strong, satisfactory, weak, poor, and unsatisfactory, all parties to grading would have a better understanding of the message.

"But minimal grading doesn't really solve this problem. Grades are just as ambiguous if most students get a satisfactory." Not so. Even if most students get a satisfactory and thus the grade is given to a wide level of performances (which will tend to happen), the result is *not* so ambiguous as the present grading system. For we will have *clearly communicated* that the grade has this wide range of meanings through the use of an honest word (satisfactory) and because we have used a limited scale. We won't have the ambiguity of the present situation where no one knows whether B means satisfactory or not satisfactory or whether B is being used for a wide or a restricted range of performances.

"Some teachers will probably still give mostly excellent or strong." This need not be seen as a problem, because teachers have, as it were, signed their names to those *words*: they are certifying that the majority of performances in the class are in fact excellent or strong or honors level. Surely it can happen that most of the performances on a paper or even in a course are in truth excellent or strong—and we want to sign our name honestly to that report. In the present situation, when a teacher gives mostly A-'s and B+'s, no one knows whether she is saying, "This was a remarkable outcome," or just, "It's not too hard to get a B+ in my system." Besides, the worst grade inflation is not at the upper level but the lower level. Most teachers give passing grades and even C's to performances that they do not consider satisfactory. There would be less of this if they had to use the word satisfactory.

Giving Grades More Meaning: Using Explicit Criteria

I have been arguing that we can get students to work hard and invest themselves in certain assignments if we raise the stakes but still use minimal grading—meanwhile making strategic decisions about how high to raise the stakes, how many minimal levels to use, and where to place the bars or thresholds between levels. We won't have to struggle with the eleven levels of conventional grading, and the results will be fairer. Why struggle to distinguish between a B and a B-, giving ourselves more work and our students more occasions for resentment, when the resulting decision lacks not just meaning but fairness.

Nevertheless, if the stakes are high there *will* be anxiety and potential argument around where we set those borderlines between satisfactory and unsatisfactory, or between satisfactory and excellent. So how do we decide how high to place the bar? How do we figure out exactly what we mean by "a satisfactory essay" or "an excellent essay"? This is where we get into head scratching with ourselves, honest disagreement with colleagues, and unpleasant arguments with students.

We can never make grading completely easy or completely fair—but in this second section, I think I can show a path toward improvement. The key is to think about the *information* or *meaning* carried by a grade.

Despite the advantages of minimal grades, we must admit that conventional grades carry *more* information. That is, conventional grades are more precise than minimal grades at telling *how well* or *how badly* students did at a task. However, this added information is not only untrustworthy; it is empty. That is, conventional grades tell nothing at all about *what it is* that the student did well or badly; the greater precision of conventional grades is utterly untrustworthy. In fact, we don't even *get* that alleged precision unless we see the range of grades for the whole class. But however bad the added information is, the fact remains that conventional grades sort students into more groups that are more finely differentiated, giving students a sense of seeing themselves as better and worse in relation to *more* of their peers. In short, however dubious the value or reliability of conventional grading, students tend at first to experience minimal grading as *taking something away from them*—and something deeply valued.

My purpose in this section is to show that we can give students *better* information or meaning in return for the bad information we take away from them. We can make minimal grades more meaningful than conventional grades if we can tell students what they are actually weak, satisfactory, or excellent *at*—and also show them that our minimal grades are actually fairer. To do so, we need to work out the *criteria* for our minimal grades.

For low stakes assignments, criteria don't matter so much. Still, it's not hard to come up with workable criteria that are easy to apply—so that papers can be graded quickly and with no head scratching—and in the case of large classes can even be perfunctorily checked. Here is what a typical handout might say about the criteria for weekly *thinkpieces*.

> *To be Acceptable the piece must be at least 750 words. You don't have to have a unified essay with a single thesis or point. And you don't have to be right in everything you say about the course material. I invite you to speculate and pursue hunches. But you must seriously wrestle with or engage the academic material in the week's reading and the topic or issue that I specify. Informal, colloquial writing is fine, but it must be clear to me as reader. Handwriting is acceptable—even a few scratch-outs and write-ins are fine—as long as the piece is neat enough to make it genuinely easy to read.*

One could add other features to the criteria: for example, that students quote a passage from the reading and work with the quote or that students be more or less right in what they say about the course material—or at least not badly wrong. (This last criterion would require more careful reading by the teacher.)

With high stakes assignments, however, we see the greatest need and the greatest opportunity to make grades carry more genuinely useful information or meaning. If we specify and use criteria for high stakes minimal grading, we will vastly reduce uncertainty for us, and resentment, hostility, or discouragement for students.

Using Criteria But Not Grading Each One. Figuring out our criteria and spelling them out publicly doesn't mean we have to give a grade on each criterion on each paper. It's when we *don't* spell out criteria publicly that we have the most obligation to spell out individual reasons on each paper why it got its grade. One of our options is to tell students ahead of time what we are looking for in the papers and then give only a single minimal grade. We need this option particularly when we have a large class that doesn't center on writing and we have little or no help in teaching, or when we want to assign a lot of papers.

There is a traditional and crude distinction between *form* and *content* that many teachers use quite successfully (despite some criticism of it as old fashioned or even theoretically suspect). For example, one might explain one's criteria for a high stakes essay in a large course as follows:

> I will grade these important essays on a three-level scale, unsatisfactory, satisfactory, excellent. I will count roughly two-thirds for content and one-third for form. By content, I mean thinking, analysis, support, examples [or one might talk about specific concepts or issues in the topic]. By form, I mean clarity and correctness.

Teachers sometimes break out these two broad criteria into four more explicit ones: correct understanding of course material, good ideas and interesting thinking, clarity, mechanics.

These are traditional but sturdy, workable criteria. Yet of course, we can work out our own criteria according to our own tastes—perhaps changing them on different papers. (Here are just a few of the diverse criteria I have seen faculty members use in grading: analysis of quantitative data, persuasion, researching new information, accuracy with sources, applying course concepts to new situations, effective revision from an early draft, effective or clear organization, establishing an appropriate relationship with readers, clear and lively voice, correct use of citation conventions, copyediting.)[2]

When we spell out our criteria in public—in an announcement or on a handout—we are making our grades carry more information or meaning than they usually do, even if we give nothing but a minimal grade. All too often, grading criteria are left tacit and mysterious. Also, when we spell out criteria in public, we usually grade more fairly. That is, when we lay out our criteria, we are not so likely to be unduly swayed if one particular feature of the writing is terribly weak or strong. (Research shows that teachers tend to get annoyed by papers that are full of grammar and spelling mistakes and nonstandard dialect, and consequently overlook virtues in content or reasoning in such papers.)

Giving Grades on Individual Criteria: Using a Grid. If we don't have too many students, we may discover that we *can* tell students how they did on each criterion. The principle of minimal grading comes to our rescue here. For just as it isn't so hard to read through a set of papers and merely pick out ones that are *notably weak* or *notably strong,* so it isn't so hard merely to note if an essay is notably weak or strong on the criteria we have named as important. Thus we might use a kind of grid and the "grade" on the high stakes paper might look like this (using traditional criteria):

CORRECT UNDERSTANDING OF COURSE MATERIAL: Excellent
GOOD IDEAS AND INTERESTING THINKING: Satisfactory
CLARITY: Satisfactory
MECHANICS: Satisfactory
OVERALL: Excellent

Notice that the overall grade is excellent but it is based on three satisfactories and only one excellent. That is, the use of criteria doesn't oblige us to be rigid or simpleminded in evaluating. Most teachers decide that content counts more than form. By noting strengths and weaknesses on a crude scale using multiple criteria, we give far more meaning and clarity to three-level grades than students get from the eleven levels of conventional grades. Yet doing so is usually not much harder than trying to figure out those conventional grades—and if the class is large, we can get away without writing a *verbal* comment. In truth, these crude notations on criteria are often more helpful than most of our verbal comments.

The most important advantage of this extensive use of criteria is that students at last get some substantive feedback on what they did well or badly. Most students will probably get an overall grade of satisfactory, so they will benefit enormously from knowing which dimensions of their papers were notably weak or strong. And the students with grades of unsatisfactory badly need more particular feedback—not just from having their most egregious sins named, but just as importantly, from getting some encouragement by seeing that not *everything* was unsatisfactory.[3]

Conclusion: Less of the Vertical, More of the Horizontal

Everything I'm saying in this chapter can be seen in terms of a contrast between what I call a *vertical* and a *horizontal* emphasis in grading. We see the vertical emphasis in conventional A through F grades. (We see even steeper verticality when faculty members grade essays on a scale of 1 to 100—as they do in many law schools.) Conventional grades distinguish eleven levels of *pure quality*—quality that is entirely undefined and unarticulated: conventional grades constitute nothing but a vertical stack of levels—each one defined in no other way than "better than the one below, worse than the one above"; it's all numbers, no words; a yea/boo meter with eleven markings. This pure numerical verticality with no words or concepts is the source of the difficulty, disputes, and untrustworthiness in conventional grading. It is enormously hard to define or specify which essays should get an A and which ones an A- when we have no words or concepts or criteria. ("For an A, your paper can't be just *really* good, it must be *really really* good.")

I can summarize this chapter as two different movements away from pure verticality:

1. Minimal grading doesn't add anything horizontal; it merely means *less* verticality: only three or so levels instead of eleven. That is, minimal grading doesn't add any horizontal element—it is still nothing but a plain vertical line. But there is less relentless obsession with multiplicity of vertical distinctions. And defining the verticality with words or concepts (satisfactory, excellent) rather than just numbers gives a bit of relief from the verticality of pure numbers.

2. The use of criteria actually *adds* a horizontal dimension to grading. We are specifying two or more criteria at right angles to the vertical line of pure undefined quality. The fullest use of criteria involves making multiple judgments of quality. But even if we just specify criteria—naming them but not giving grades on them—we are still adding a significant horizontal dimension.

The choice between a vertical emphasis and a horizontal emphasis is stark. With the vertical emphasis, we are making a *single* difficult, sophisticated, evaluative decision along a *single* scale with multiple levels—but no words or definitions are involved. With a horizontal emphasis, we are making multiple decisions on multiple criteria—which are named—and the decisions are simpler, easier, and more believable. With the vertical emphasis, all the multiplicity is piled on top of itself—and undefined; with the horizontal emphasis, the multiplicity is laid out side by side—and defined.

We can also think of this as a choice between working with *quality* and *qualities*. To traffic in quality is to deal with a pure, unnamed, mystical essence. To traffic in qualities is to deal with admittedly crude and inexact entities—but at least readers can see what we are trying to evaluate.

My argument then is that if we use minimal grades, we are merely using less of the vertical dimension, but in doing so, we will make grading simpler for us, less questionable or dubious for students, and less disruptive of the teaching and learning climate. And if we use criteria and actually add some of the horizontal dimension, we will also make our grades much more meaningful, less magic or mystical. And we will be giving students valuable feedback on the strengths and weaknesses in their writing—feedback that they don't get from conventional grades.

Notes

1. Here are some activities that are often specified in contracts: attend class regularly; turn in assignments on time (to increase the benefit from discussions and lectures); revise cer-

tain papers; get rid of mistakes in spelling and grammar on final drafts; give written feedback on certain drafts to other members of the class; get written feedback from other members of the class (also perhaps people not in the class); turn in a *process log* with drafts and papers (containing elements such as a clear précis, a discussion of the writing process, an estimate of the strengths and weaknesses, and questions for the reader to answer in giving feedback).

It's probably most common to use a contract for a course grade of B—and then fall back on the question of excellent quality in deciding higher grades. But some teachers make contracts for higher grades containing additional contract requirements such as these: with each major paper, submit an outline that accurately shows the logic of the argument—the relation between main points, subsidiary points, and evidence; write a report on a book, lecture, movie, play not assigned for the course—showing how it sheds light on the course material; meet outside of class in small groups for certain tasks; make a presentation to the class or to some members—perhaps outside of class time; interview someone outside the class who has important expertise or experience in the realm we are studying—and make a report; give or get additional feedback on certain drafts; re-revise certain papers. Here are some more intriguing and speculative ways that teachers have tried to specify *activities* in writing to try to force students to write more productively: make sure that certain essays contain an element of exploration or perplexity or questioning—rather than just a summary of material or just an explanation of what is indisputable or obvious; certain essays must demonstrate the intersection of theoretical academic issues and some part of your personal experience—and how they shed light on each other.

2. A note about working out one's criteria: when students ask me, "What are you looking for?" I sometimes feel some annoyance (though I don't think my reaction is quite fair). But I enjoy it when *I* ask the question of myself: "What actually *are* the features in a piece of writing that make me value it?" If I try to answer this question in an insecure, normative way, I tie myself in knots: "What *ought* I to value in student essays?" But we are professionals in our fields, and so we get to ask the question in an *empirical* way: "What *do* I value in the writing in my field?" For there is no correct answer to the question, "What is good writing?"

This process of empirical self-examination can be intellectually fascinating. We learn to notice more clearly how we read—and this can even prompt some change in how we read. For example, some faculty members discover that they are judging on fewer criteria than they realized (for example, mostly on the basis of correct restatement of textbook and lecture material and correct mechanics)—and this realization leads them to attend to other criteria. Or they discover that they use different criteria for student writing than for professional writing (for example, in student writing they disapprove of the use of first-person writing or personal anecdote, but in published professional writing in their field they value it).

3. I need to add a note here about the vexed criterion of *mechanics* or *correctness* or *spelling and grammar*. Some teachers give it lots of weight—others not very much. Both positions are defensible. In working out my own view, I am helped again by invoking the *empirical* approach and asking myself, "How much do I value mechanics or correctness in the writing in my field?" The empirical principle helps me to see there is no single answer. That is, I don't value correctness very much in exploratory writing, drafts, informal reports, or e-mail—or at least not unless mistakes really impede my reading. I certainly don't care much about correctness in my own writing till I get to good drafts for readers I don't know. But I am put off when I notice mistakes in published writing, and so I work at correctness when I give good drafts to strangers or a wide audience.

I have derived my grading policy from this analysis. I don't use correctness as a criterion on drafts and informal writing, but I count it heavily on important papers that I treat as final drafts. (Usually, I set up assignments so that there is a draft due well before the final due date—even if I don't read it. I tend to treat the draft as a kind of medium stakes assignment: it doesn't have to be done well—but the punishment is heavy if it is not done on time. This helps the high stakes paper a great deal.) For example, I might say that a high stakes final draft is not eligible for the overall grade of excellent unless it has an excellent on correctness; and that a satisfactory is out of the question unless it is satisfactory on correctness.

Some students call this policy too stiff, and some colleagues say it isn't fair to students for whom English is a second language (ESL students). But it's workable once I make my reasoning clear to students: "I never penalize you for mistakes on drafts or on tests where you can't revise and get help. I'm not requiring you to know how to copyedit well—*on your own*—*without help*. But I *am* requiring you to learn to do whatever is necessary to get important papers well copyedited. Few of you can do it without help; *I* can't do it without help. Get help. What I am insisting on is an ability you will need for most teachers and most jobs: to do whatever is needed to turn in clean copy." It turns out that most ESL students are better at understanding the logic of this policy than most native speakers. I tell my students, "Here is another schizophrenia. On the one hand, I'm trying to teach you how to write on drafts without even thinking about correctness. On the other hand, I'm trying to teach you to worry a great deal about correctness in the last stages of preparing an important final draft." I'm not saying that this policy makes everything simple. I usually give students one "warning": the first time they turn in an important final draft that is badly copyedited, I usually just stop reading, reject it, count it as late, and say, "This isn't acceptable"—and let them fix it with only a small penalty. (They all get to have one late paper.) After that, I try to be as tough as I am pretending to be, for I believe they need to learn how to turn in clean copy.

References

Belanoff, P., and Dickson, M. *Portfolios: Process and Product.* Portsmouth, N.H.: Heinemann, Boynton/Cook, 1991.

White, E. "Language and Reality in Writing Assessment." *College Composition and Communication,* 1990, *41,* 187–200.

Yancey, K. B. *Portfolios in the Writing Classroom: An Introduction.* Urbana, Ill.: National Council of Teachers of English, 1992.

PETER ELBOW is professor of English and director of the writing program at the University of Massachusetts, Amherst.

This chapter suggests ways in which faculty development programs can improve student learning and foster more effective teaching through writing-to-learn programs and activities.

The Role of Faculty Development Programs in Helping Teachers to Improve Student Learning Through Writing

Elizabeth Ann Caldwell, Mary Deane Sorcinelli

In academic environments faced with changing enrollment patterns, increased demands for accountability, declining financial resources, and faculties adversely affected by these and other conditions, faculty development professionals have had to devise ever more versatile ways to improve the quality of undergraduate teaching and learning. In an analysis of a wide variety of faculty development activities in many different institutions—large and small, public and private, well endowed and financially troubled—Eble and McKeachie (1986) found that writing-across-the-curriculum workshops were among the most frequently offered faculty development activities and were rated among the most effective by program directors.

Our experience at the Center For Teaching (CFT), the faculty development office at the University of Massachusetts, Amherst, confirms this phenomenon. Workshops and seminars that help faculty to improve student learning through writing are among the best attended and most highly rated of our annual events. Our experience also shows that teaching development programs can work as partners with writing programs to improve teaching and learning.

Linkages Between Writing, Learning, and Faculty Development

Our campus's Center For Teaching (CFT) and its Writing Program, which from its early years has had a well-developed writing-across-the-curriculum component, have enjoyed a lasting and creative partnership starting shortly after both had taken shape, in the mid- to late 1980s. In fact, one of the CFT's first projects was a Lilly Teaching Fellows seminar entitled "Using Writing in the Classroom," conducted by the Writing Program director and a fellow from the Department of Landscape Architecture and Regional Planning, who demonstrated ways of using writing to enhance learning in large classes. Other offerings followed, as each year the center enlarged the scope of its programming to reflect just how central writing is to the activities of academic life and to respond to faculty requests for support in using writing as a mode of learning in their courses.

In part because of its relationship with the Writing Program, the CFT has thought of the connections between writing and learning as integral to its approaches to faculty development. However, the key in its practice has been to focus on writing as a way of helping students to become more active and self-aware learners and as a way of helping teachers to gain more insight into students' thinking and learning processes. Thus most of our programming is not built on a view of writing as disciplinary enculturation; this view we feel is more richly conceived and more aptly served by writing programs and by the departments and disciplines themselves than by faculty development organizations. Our premise is a different but complementary view of writing as a mode of knowing, of learning. In this respect, writing-to-learn activities reach beyond disciplinary boundaries to address learning processes themselves and teachers' roles in those processes.

The critical difference for us, then, has been that rather than helping teachers to enable their students to write like practitioners of a discipline—like historians, nurses, anthropologists, or biologists—we help teachers incorporate into their work with students writing that will help students to learn the content, perspectives, attitudes, modes of thought and inquiry, and ethos of their fields. The focus is on the students and on the learning, rather than on the written artifacts themselves.

Writing-to-Learn Programs for Faculty

The rubric writing-to-learn often refers to short ungraded focusing or exploratory exercises that students complete in class, writing to and for themselves "in the interest of collecting their thoughts and getting them down on paper where they can be inspected, extended, connected, organized, and revised" (Erickson and Strommer, 1991, p. 115). However, as the chapters in this volume illustrate, the spectrum of practices and points of view represented by the rubric are actually quite broad. Over time, three categories of activities that reflect this breadth have evolved at the CFT: direct programming whose explicit purpose is to aid faculty and teaching assistants in using writing to help students to learn, programming in which writing-to-learn is embedded in larger focal concepts, and individual or departmental consultations.

Direct Programming. The response to the first collaboration with the Writing Program was so strong and positive that the two organizations joined with the University Writing Committee the following year to present a two-part series for a campuswide audience, "Writing to Learn: Using Writing to Foster Student Learning." The first session focused on creating writing assignments and the second on responding to students' writing. The presenters at both sessions represented a variety of disciplines, class sizes, levels, and types of courses. In order to provide participants with a chance to discuss their specific questions and problems, each workshop included small working groups led by teams of faculty presenters and Writing Program personnel.

That year the center also sponsored a workshop to help faculty to write more productively and successfully in their professional lives. This session was based on the popular text *Professors as Writers* (Boice, 1990). A more comprehensive and theoretical view of the connections between writing and learning was offered through a forum entitled "Issues and Conflicts in Writing Across the Curriculum: Directions for the 1990s and Beyond." The CFT and Writing Program cosponsored this session with a local higher education consortium. This discussion, based on the Public Broadcasting Service's teleconference featuring national leaders in the field of writing across the curriculum, was facilitated by a multidisciplinary panel of faculty from several colleges and our university.

Subsequent years have produced other, often unique formats as well. "Faculty as Writers," a four-part writing workshop in which faculty work together on their own professional and scholarly writing, has been offered for three consecutive years and has been consistently oversubscribed. Bringing in their own works-in-progress for review allowed teachers to gain a firsthand perspective on what writing is like for their students and how it relates to the unique features of their own disciplines. Participants have had high praise for the series, citing the value of a supportive writing group in helping them meet individual goals, in providing an interdisciplinary audience, and in influencing teaching as well as scholarship.

Frequently, the actual practices of teachers in different disciplines have been the subjects of workshops. A presentation by faculty in the Departments of Physics and Astronomy, Psychology, and Art, all of whom had participated in their departments' Junior Year Writing Programs, offered rationales for course design and pedagogy, and discussed the outcomes and rewards of their efforts. Another offering focused on the uses of writing assignments as tools to help students explore conceptual problems and was presented jointly by faculty from the School of Management and the Departments of Landscape Architecture and Regional Planning, Physics and Astronomy, and English, as well as the Writing Program. They demonstrated how writing can be used to generate conceptual thinking, to act as the foundation for collaborative learning groups, and to model problem solving in class.

Embedded Programming. While programming aimed overtly at providing teachers with a rationale and strategies for using writing-to-learn will reach those who have an interest in the subject, the principles that underlie these sessions can find their way into more broadly conceived programs as well. For example, the annual Teaching Assistant Orientation offered in cooperation with the Graduate School and the Provost's Office features a session entitled "Responding to Writing: A Workshop." This session suggests methods for providing timely, instructive, and efficient responses that are appropriate to the nature of an assignment, and for evaluating fairly. A fall semester TA development seminar, "Evaluating Student Work," addressed issues of evaluating and grading both objectively scored tests and qualitatively evaluated formats that use writing, such as essay exams, research papers, and journals.

Workshops on active learning, teaching with case study methodology, and multicultural communication in the classroom all have featured short written problem solving in groups. Sessions on cooperative learning and collaborative writing, in particular, emphasized the roles of writing in encouraging students to engage with course material more fully and to take responsibility for their own learning. In none of these sessions was the subject writing itself; rather participants examined their colleagues' strategies and experienced for themselves how writing can be used to accomplish learning objectives.

Consultations. It is common for us to incorporate recommendations related to writing into individual consultations, because it is such a versatile and adaptable teaching tool. Here is a selection of scenarios that illustrate the range of pedagogical aims that writing can address:

• A professor from the psychology department wanted to better focus student attention on a topic at the start of her large lecture classes. We suggested that at the beginning of each lecture she ask students to write briefly about one of three aspects of the subject: what they knew about the subject, what opinions they held about it, or what their personal experiences with the subject had been. For example, before a lecture on adolescent development, she would ask students to reflect on their own development and describe some personal "markers" of their own entrance into adolescence. Students then shared their experiences in pairs, selected pairs reported themes to the whole class, and the teacher finally collected writings and later graded them with a check or check plus. Beyond focusing student attention in preparation for the lecture, beginning-of-class writing settled down this very large class and helped in assessing attendance—collecting the pieces let the instructor know who was absent that day. More importantly, as they wrote, students were placed in the role of *knowers*. They inventoried their own knowledge, saw themselves as persons with knowledge, and then were prepared and able to bring this knowledge to the subsequent interaction with the teacher, in which they could connect what they knew with what others knew.

• A professor in a general education science course was concerned about student passivity and inattention. He wanted to break out of the seventy-five-minute lecture routine and more actively involve students. After several experiments, we came up with this strategy: he first divided the lecture into fifteen- to twenty-minute blocks. At the end of each block, he listed one or two questions on the board—for example, "Identify and describe two or three reasons why biotechnology is important for developing countries." His questions varied from topic to topic, of course, but they often called for an understanding of a fundamental concept just covered or the making of a connection between the content and student experience. Students wrote responses and shared them in pairs, raising questions and identifying issues, and then the class returned to the lecture format.

• A history professor was discouraged with student preparation for seminar discussion. He developed a *reading response sheet* that students filled out at home for each reading assignment and carried into class for discussion. Questions on the response sheets included:

> *What do you anticipate learning from this reading, just looking at it for the first time?*
>> *When did the author write? To what audience? Under what personal/professional circumstances?*
> *What was the author trying to accomplish by writing?*
> *On what topics do you trust the author? On what not at all? Where do you take the author with a grain of salt?*
> *Take any one of the guiding questions for the course from the first page of our course syllabus. How does this reading help answer it?*

In our end-of-semester interviews with students, they rated the reading response sheet as one of the most valuable aids to learning in the course. They found that such writing helped them to become "active readers," to "reflect on and analyze what they were reading," and to "stimulate class discussion." Students pointed to the questions that related back to the guiding questions for the course as especially helpful.

• A professor in environmental sciences was concerned that students were not performing well on tests, particularly on material covered in lectures. We introduced her to the *minute paper,* "a quick and simple way to collect written feedback on student learning" (Angelo and Cross, 1992, p. 148; also see the discussion of freewriting in Chapter Five). She began the practice of handing out index cards at the end of each class, asking students to take two or three minutes to jot down the most important thing they learned during class and what questions remained unanswered. She then collected and reviewed the cards to check on what students understood and where they might have been confused, and summarized and discussed the results at the start of the next class. These minute papers allowed her to quickly check how well her students were learning what she was teaching and whether she needed to make adjustments in content, scheduling, or materials. Also, getting the instructor's feedback on their minute papers helped students learn how to distinguish major points from details and ensured that students' questions or concerns would be raised and answered in time to facilitate further learning.

• Discouraged with the outcome of high stakes paper assignments, a humanities professor turned each step of a large assignment into a smaller assignment. For example, in a course on third-world films he asked students to turn in a *freewriting idea paper,* an outline, a bibliography, and then a first draft. By making cumulative assignments, he helped students work through the process of composing a long paper more effectively (see Chapter Six).

• The College of Engineering wished to examine both the content and the teaching of the junior-year writing component of their curriculum for undergraduate majors. Personnel from the college, the Writing Program, and the CFT worked together to design evaluations to determine what kinds of writing and instruction were most useful to students as aspiring engineers. This review led to a revision of the junior-year writing program to include more computer-based assignments, more frequent and shorter papers, more rewriting, and more discipline-specific readings and writing projects.

As these examples show, our faculty have found writing-to-learn particularly useful at three key junctures in the learning process. Early in the process, writing can stimulate interest and open avenues for making material personally meaningful as students *prepare* for lecture, reading, discussion, or performance tasks. Later, it can focus, extend, and challenge students' thinking as they *engage* in purposeful inquiry. And throughout the process, it can enable students to *reflect on, synthesize,* or *assess* texts, experiences, or their own thinking. Like many chapters in this collection, the kinds of consultations just described embody the "dialectic" that Elbow describes between low and high stakes writing (see Chapter Eleven). The experiences of these faculty also show that writing can be used to learn many things, from the content of texts or the matrices of disciplines to individuals' personal perspectives and the impact of these perspectives on others.

Lessons Learned

Perhaps the core success of writing-to-learn programs rests upon the fact that faculty come to see such activities as helping them to teach more effectively and helping their students to learn. We suggest six general outcomes, based on nearly a decade of experience, that may have value to other campuses.

Writing-to-learn programs provide opportunities for faculty and TAs to develop new teaching skills. Initially, we introduced writing-to-learn activities to our Lilly Teaching Fellows, all of whom were untenured faculty. Many felt uncertain about how to improve their teaching and typically had received little guidance in graduate school or from colleagues about creative and effective approaches to teaching. Writing-to-learn activities directly responded to their need to learn more about teaching. In using writing in the classroom, many fellows reported concrete changes in their teaching: they rewrote syllabi to place more emphasis on writing and to require more of it, both formal and informal, and gained greater confidence that they could work usefully with students' writing. In addition, they reported that such activities heightened their sensitivity to student differences and helped them listen to students in ways that aided in building a community of learners in the classroom. Based on such positive responses, we then enlisted Writing Program faculty, Lilly Teaching Fellows, and senior faculty mentors to act as presenters at campuswide workshops. In this way, we were able to create forums for the exchange of writing-to-learn ideas among faculty across disciplines and career stages.

Writing-to-learn activities affect instructors' approaches to teaching and learning. Writing-to-learn programs often lead faculty members from discussion of a particular activity to broader discussions of how they actually do their teaching and how their students learn. On our campus, conversations at writing-to-learn programs quickly spilled over into dialogues on larger issues such as student learning styles and the value of alternative teaching methods. When they became aware, for instance, that writing-to-learn techniques could help students to understand course content or prepare for class, instructors began to assign short writing homework that helped students to develop better note-taking strategies and provided a complement to out-of-class reading. When they were persuaded that active learning activities improved student learning, instructors began to break up lectures with short periods of writing in order to focus, challenge, or explore lecture concepts. When they became convinced of the critical importance of practice and review in student learning, instructors began to use such strategies as the minute paper to help students to reflect on what they had learned and to gather prompt feedback on learning outcomes.

Historically in teaching development programs, we have focused more on the act of teaching than on students' learning, except in discussions of assessment. Yet unlike lectures or class discussions, students' writing gives us a window into their thought processes as learners. Perhaps another reason why writing-to-learn activities fit so nicely with faculty development is that writing shifts the focus to learning: writing is *learning made visible*. And once faculty begin to think about students as learners, the road to good teaching is smoother.

Writing-to-learn activities provide a forum for sharing the talent, perspectives, and expertise of instructors from all quarters of the campus. In one of our early campuswide programs, we brought in an outside consultant with expertise in writing. This program was an unqualified success, providing valuable stimulation and insights. At the same time, over the years we have had at least as great success with the use of local talent. The most common—and probably most successful—use of local expertise has been in workshops in which participants not only learn about but actually try out writing-to-learn activities used by colleagues from different disciplines. Faculty members come to see such peers as highly credible; colleagues from across the disciplines bring a sense of authenticity, of being anchored in an individual classroom, to what otherwise might be rather hypothetical advice. Finally, use of local talent encourages the development of teaching skills in an interdisciplinary and collaborative environment and provides some modicum of recognition for the good teachers and good teaching practices that flourish, often unnoticed, across our institutions.

Writing-to-learn activities provide opportunities for professional development in ways that integrate scholarship and teaching. Too often academe sets up a teaching-versus-research dichotomy. Writing-to-learn programs can affirm the natural and positive connections between scholarship and teaching. For example, as mentioned earlier, we offer an annual "Faculty as Writers" series that has two goals: enabling faculty to be more productive in their own professional and scholarly writing and helping them learn how to use writing more effectively in their courses. This program has been highly successful because it offers help in the kinds of writing that faculty identify as important for their own development as well as for the success of their students. Faculty participants report not only gaining confidence in teaching writing and using it in classes but also gaining confidence in their own writing. By linking the writing of faculty and the writing of students, we are able to help faculty to blend and combine teaching and scholarship in concrete ways, adding to their power as writers and as teachers of writing.

Writing-to-learn activities increase communication about teaching and learning both within and between departments and colleges. Especially at larger institutions, faculty have few links with colleagues in other disciplines that are not based on doing the work of the institution, such as serving on committees. Faculty development activities, and particularly writing workshops and seminars, constitute such a link. These programs offer new and original ideas, provide intellectual stimulation around teaching issues, and create a sense of community that helps to break down the isolation felt by many faculty in their roles as teachers. When we evaluate such sessions on our campus, many faculty report that the most important outcome is the increase in communication, interaction, and collaboration across departmental and disciplinary boundaries, allowing teachers to see some of the pandisciplinary features of good teaching.

Writing-to-learn activities enable faculty to do a better job without a major increase in time spent on correcting and grading papers. Numerous studies of faculty indicate that "not enough time to do . . . work" is a primary stressor throughout the academic career (Boice, 1992; Gmelch, 1993; Sorcinelli and Austin, 1992). Writing-to-learn activities not only foster greater effectiveness in student learning but also permit greater efficiency in teaching. Strategies such as those illustrated by many of the chapters in this sourcebook can give instructors the insight into student thinking and learning that will allow them to offer appropriate support and direction and provide more and better feedback to students without greater expenditure of time.

Writing-to-learn activities promote linkages between writing programs and faculty development programs that are beneficial to both. Writing programs and teaching development programs can work together to improve student learning. Such partnerships can help to build alliances among campus constituencies that might otherwise operate in isolation. Collaborative activities allow writing programs to promote writing *as learning,* not only as a means to assess what students *have learned.* They also allow writing programs to counteract the belief, widely held outside of English departments, that the work of writing teachers is teaching grammar, diction, and mechanics.

Beyond guaranteeing successful programming, partnerships with writing programs encourage teaching and faculty development centers to incorporate writing into all the operations of the center, offering a practical model of writing-to-learn. For example, we do this by gathering written, qualitative feedback on all CFT programs and events and by trying out writing-to-learn activities (for example, freewriting, journals, and minute papers) as part of learning *about* teaching in all of our programs.

Conclusion

Many faculty development organizations in institutions large and small adhere to a philosophy that holds that "teaching excellence has both general and discipline-specific features . . . that the ways in which academics stimulate inquiry, generate knowledge, and present information are content-driven. At the same time, there are certain general features of good teaching—establishing and communicating clear learning objectives, actively involving students in learning, and evaluating performance in ways that are prompt and that accurately reflect goals—which are common to all disciplines" (*Annual Report,* 1996, p. 1).

These principles can be seen at work in the earlier chapters of this volume, which reveal how profoundly writing assignments and activities, as well as responses to students' writing, are part of the intellectual "economy" of higher education. Put simply, writing-to-learn programming in its many forms can open up new opportunities to create linkages, cross boundaries, foster new skills and attitudes, and develop collegial and collaborative environments for teaching and learning on any campus.

References

Angelo, T. A., and Cross, K. P. *Classroom Assessment Techniques: A Handbook for College Teachers.* (2nd ed.) San Francisco: Jossey-Bass, 1993.
Annual Report. Amherst: Center For Teaching, University of Massachusetts, 1995.
Boice, R. *Professors as Writers.* Stillwater, Okla.: New Forums Press, 1990.
Boice, R. *The New Faculty Member: Supporting and Fostering Professional Development.* San Francisco: Jossey-Bass, 1992.
Eble, K. E., and McKeachie, W. J. *Improving Undergraduate Education Through Faculty Development: An Analysis of Effective Programs and Practices.* San Francisco: Jossey-Bass, 1986.
Erickson, B. L., and Strommer, D. W. *Teaching College Freshmen.* San Francisco: Jossey-Bass, 1991.
Gmelch, W. H. *Coping with Faculty Stress.* Thousand Oaks, Calif.: Sage, 1993.
Sorcinelli, M. D., and Austin, A. E. (eds.). *Developing New and Junior Faculty.* New Directions for Teaching and Learning, no. 50. San Francisco: Jossey-Bass, 1992.

ELIZABETH ANN CALDWELL is composition specialist and project director at the Center For Teaching at the University of Massachusetts, Amherst.

MARY DEANE SORCINELLI is associate provost for faculty development and director of the Center For Teaching at the University of Massachusetts, Amherst.

INDEX

ORDERING INFORMATION

NEW DIRECTIONS FOR TEACHING AND LEARNING is a series of paperback books that presents ideas and techniques for improving college teaching, based both on the practical expertise of seasoned instructors and on the latest research findings of educational and psychological researchers. Books in the series are published quarterly in Spring, Summer, Fall, and Winter and are available for purchase by subscription as well as by single copy.

SUBSCRIPTIONS cost $52.00 for individuals (a savings of 35 percent over single-copy prices) and $79.00 for institutions, agencies, and libraries. Please do not send institutional checks for personal subscriptions. Standing orders are accepted. Prices subject to change. (For subscriptions outside of North America, add $7.00 for shipping via surface mail or $25.00 for air mail. Orders *must be prepaid* in U.S. dollars by check drawn on a U.S. bank or charged to VISA, MasterCard, or American Express.)

SINGLE COPIES cost $20.00 plus shipping (see below) when payment accompanies order. California, New Jersey, New York, and Washington, D.C., residents please include appropriate sales tax. Canadian residents add GST and any local taxes. Billed orders will be charged shipping and handling. No billed shipments to post office boxes. (Orders from outside North America *must be prepaid* in U.S. dollars by check drawn on a U.S. bank or charged to VISA, MasterCard, or American Express.)

SHIPPING (SINGLE COPIES ONLY): $10.00 and under, add $2.50; to $20.00, add $3.50; to $50.00, add $4.50; to $75.00, add $5.50; to $100.00, add $6.50; to $150.00, add $7.50; over $150.00, add $8.50.

DISCOUNTS FOR QUANTITY ORDERS are available. Please write to the address below for information.

ALL ORDERS must include either the name of an individual or an official purchase order number. Please submit your order as follows:
   Subscriptions: specify series and year subscription is to begin
   Single copies: include individual title code (such as TL54)

MAIL ALL ORDERS TO:
   Jossey-Bass Publishers
   350 Sansome Street
   San Francisco, CA 94104-1342

FOR SUBSCRIPTION SALES OUTSIDE OF THE UNITED STATES, CONTACT:
   any international subscription agency or Jossey-Bass directly.